HELLBOY™

THE COMPANION

HELLBOY™

THE COMPANION

STEPHEN WEINER
JASON HALL
VICTORIA BLAKE

with additional material by
MIKE MIGNOLA

*Featuring the art of Mike Mignola, Guy Davis, Ryan Sook,
Duncan Fegredo, Jason Shawn Alexander, and Paul Azaceta*

DARK HORSE BOOKS®

To Craig Shaw Gardner, Chris Couch, and Denis Kitchen.
—*Stephen Weiner*

To my fellow *Hellboy* fanatics and continuity geeks everywhere who were dying
to know what Hellboy was doing in . . . oh, say . . . June of 1961. This is for us!
—*Jason Hall*

For Mike M. and Scott A.—for the privilege of watching the creative mind at play.
—*Victoria Blake*

Publisher *Mike Richardson*
Editors *Scott Allie and Rachel Edidin*
Book Designer *Heidi Whitcomb*
Art Director *Lia Ribacchi*
Special Thanks to *John Arcudi, Robyn Fleming, Christopher Golden, Jason Hvam, Matt Dryer, Denis Kitchen,
Jonell Napper, Dash Robb, Samantha Robertson, Patrick Thorpe, Alison Stump, and Steve Jackson Games.*
Cover Artists *Mike Mignola with Dave Stewart*

Published by
Dark Horse Books
A division of Dark Horse Comics, Inc.
10956 SE Main Street
Milwaukie, OR 97222

darkhorse.com
hellboy.com

To find a comics shop in your area,
call the Comic Shop Locator Service toll-free at 1-888-266-4226

First Edition: May 2008
ISBN 978-1-59307-655-9

10 9 8 7 6 5 4 3 2 1

Printed in USA

CONTENTS

INTRODUCTION

by Scott Allie

O nce upon a time, *Hellboy* was mainly something that existed in phone calls between Mike Mignola and me, the only physical evidence of which was fewer than a dozen comic books. Everything that needed to be known about the character was spelled out, repeated, confirmed, and expanded upon in those daily calls that usually lasted over an hour. These were relatively early days for me at Dark Horse, when I was responsible for *Hellboy* and only a handful of other books. But if I try to compare modern times to those days for Mignola, I'm looking at a whole different degree of innocence lost. When we were doing *Wake the Devil*, for instance, there was nothing to worry about but those five issues, and all we needed to do, from the minute *Wolves of St. August* was done until we launched into *Wake*, was explore that story, go over every scene, every character, back and forth and again, to make sure it was just right.

Mike still devotes that kind of care to each story, and we still have daily phone calls that occupy a good portion of each afternoon or morning—sometimes both—but we have a lot of other things to worry about. There's the merchandise that he keeps an eye on, making sure that every toy and game and tchotchke faithfully executes the Hellboy vision. That can be a hard thing. Recently, one licensee needed to be reminded again and again that material from the movie is *not* the same as material from the comic, that in the comic Liz and Hellboy are not in love, and that Abe doesn't spend his days in a fish tank reading books on pedestals. The things you have to worry about.

These days, we also spend a good part of the day talking about the books that Mike's not drawing, like *B.P.R.D.*, which after only a few years already has as many trade paperbacks as *Hellboy*, thanks largely to the hard work of Guy Davis and John Arcudi. Or we're talking about the *Abe Sapien* series, or another series featuring Trevor Bruttenholm, set in the 1940s. Mike won't draw those, but we go through the same in-depth conversations about the stories that we did about *Wake the Devil*.

In the old days, though, we did talk about stories besides the one he was drawing right then. We'd talk about a story that he wanted to draw down the road somewhere— while working on *Wake the Devil*, we were already talking about *Conqueror Worm* and *Dark and Terrible*. If you've never heard of *Dark and Terrible*, it's because Mike never got around to drawing it—it exists only as a few pages of sketches in *The Art of Hellboy*, and now in this introduction. *Dark and Terrible* is probably gone for good—pieces of it could wind up in the next *B.P.R.D.* series, for instance, but the scope of the story doesn't fit with how things have evolved. I have to tell you, you missed out on a big story that would have added a lot to Abe Sapien as a character, and made Hellboy's world all the more mysterious.

With the current way of things, we get to do *Dark and Terrible* if it comes up. We just have to line up someone like Guy or Duncan Fegredo to draw it. But what this means, and specifically what it has to do with the book you hold in your hands, is that there's a hell of a lot more for us to keep track of. John Arcudi has now created nearly as much backstory for the Bureau as Mike has. The two of them together have certainly given us more to think about Abe Sapien than we ever had to consider before. Not to mention that when Arcudi sits down to write a story, how's he supposed to know how old Liz was when she torched her family, or what Kate did before she became a consultant and then an agent for the B.P.R.D.? Mike and I can barely keep track through our daily phone calls—and how are *you* guys supposed to keep track?

The answer is this book, where Jason Hall and Victoria Blake—working closely with Mike and me, and with help from Arcudi and *Hellboy* novelist Chris Golden—have compiled two hundred pages of information gleaned from incidental captions and flashbacks tucked away in single panels drawn as much as a decade ago. Sitting in hotel rooms and in my living room, in restaurants and on hours of phone calls, they've learned things from Mike that have never seen print. Initially proposed by Stephen Weiner as literary examination of *Hellboy*, the book has grown into so much more. Hopefully it's not just a reference book. It's intended as a book of stories, in a different format than *Chained Coffin* or *Right Hand of Doom*, but with as much art from Mike and his collaborators as we could fit. I don't think a book like it has ever been done—an all-access view, not just behind the scenes, but inside the stories, full of new detail.

There've been a lot of things indicated over the years in Mike's books, things left half-concealed in those big black shadows—things which this book begins to bring into the light. If the unnamed priest's evocative rants in *The Island* were a little bit too much for you to process, or if the mostly silent chapter issue of *Plague of Frogs* didn't exactly *tell* you Abe Sapien's origin, then this book should fill in some blanks and draw some connections.

But I would hate to think this book was going to rob Mike's world of its mystery. That was my fear when Mike and Weiner first brought it to me. Some care was taken, instead, to preserve the mystery. If *Hellboy* has always been a book that left you asking more questions than it answered, hopefully this guidebook will open up more of the mystery to you. Much of the past is yet to be revealed, and the future of the characters remains unwritten, even here. We've turned a corner in Hellboy's life, since the publication of *Conqueror Worm*, the creation of the *B.P.R.D.* series, and the upcoming release of *The Wild Hunt*. It's the next stage for him, and if the frogs or the witches are to have their way, it might be curtains for man. This book gives you more to consider about what all that means, and the secret connections between the various elements that make up Mignola's world.

I hope this book enriches your experience of this world.

—Scott Allie
En route to Texas

WHAT IS IT ABOUT HELLBOY? AN APPRECIATION

by Stephen Weiner

In 1991, when Mike Mignola provided a hasty convention sketch of a "Hellboy," he didn't realize that he'd stumbled into a world of Nazis, witchcraft, and magic, occupied by a group of supernatural characters who have dominated his attention ever since. With the publication of the first *Hellboy* comic in 1994, Mignola was able, with both drama and humor, to fuse his interests in history, fantasy, horror, folktales, and mythology with cartooning skills honed from over a decade of working in the comics industry. Hellboy's own story line begins during World War II, as a Nazi team, led by former advisor to the Russian royal family Grigori Rasputin, tries to call something up from the abyss to aid them in their quest for world domination. The Nazis and Rasputin are immediately disappointed as the child Hellboy appears not in Scotland, where they have gathered, but in a church in England where a group of occultists, sensing the Nazi plot, have led Allied troops. Hellboy is brought to America, where he becomes the ward of Professor Bruttenholm, an expert in the paranormal. Over time, Hellboy joins the Bureau for Paranormal Research and Defense and becomes its star investigator, warding off human and supernatural enemies.

THE SOURCE OF HELLBOY'S POWER

Although he is a child of hell, Hellboy chooses to reject his destiny as the Beast of the Apocalypse. No doubt thanks to his upbringing by Professor Bruttenholm, he wants to be a force for good. Hellboy's potency as a fictional character comes from this moral foundation, this contrast between his origins and his aspirations: not only does he refuse to succumb to the terrible destiny he's so often reminded of, but he devotes his life to warding off supernatural threats, big and small. Seven feet tall, with blood-red skin, a stone hand, cloven hooves, and a tail, Hellboy is quite a sight for ordinary humans, but he doesn't see himself that way. Perhaps because he was raised by humans, Hellboy sees himself as an ordinary man with a job to do. Only Hellboy doesn't fix cars, program computers, or teach third grade. His job is to keep humanity safe from the supernatural world threatening to engulf it. He and his fellow B.P.R.D. agents bring a humble, working stiff attitude to what they do. This reflects one of the most charming and distinctive traits of Mignola's work: a tendency toward understatement that paradoxically makes the weird and horrible details of his characters' work that much more startling to those of us who do not deal with frog creatures and talking corpses on a daily basis.

Hellboy, as a character, has grown over the years: for decades (the story goes) he was the lead field agent for the B.P.R.D., very involved with human beings and their problems. After defeating the Conqueror Worm at Hunte Castle, and feeling the full weight of his destiny, he left the B.P.R.D. and the world of humans, embarking on a journey to find personal meaning, which would take him deeper into the world of witches and other supernatural beings.

WHY HELLBOY NOW?

Aside from Mignola's storytelling gifts and artistic sensibilities, which have earned him every major award in the comics industry as well as the attention of book publishers and filmmakers, what makes *Hellboy* so popular? In an era when popular fiction relies heavily on fusion, *Hellboy* intricately blends the horror tale, in which the forces of darkness appear to be unstoppable, with the hero tale, in which disorder is set right by one willful protagonist. *Hellboy* also turns the standard heroic convention on its ear: Hellboy, the hero, is a child of a demon and a dead witch. Mignola plays more faithfully with the horror genre, which, like fantasy and mythology, speaks to us symbolically, isolating our fears and hopes so that we can wrestle with them from a safe distance. What's more, a careful reading of *Hellboy* reflects in part the history of American comics, and the pulp heroes that preceded them. Although Hellboy himself appears to have stepped right out of the horror genre, his personality is rooted in a particularly American corner of hero fiction—the no-nonsense detective stories first published in the pulp magazines of the 1920s and '30s. Hellboy's response to danger is decidedly American—a wisecrack followed by a powerhouse right—although his enemies are not street criminals or con men, but supernatural forces bent on destroying the world.

Another reason for *Hellboy*'s success is Mike Mignola's relationship with the *Hellboy* readership. Mignola has made himself accessible, maintaining a presence at comics conventions and inviting readers into his creative process with the liner notes that he includes in the *Hellboy* graphic novels. He's proven very forthcoming with insights into his plans and creative process through interviews and appearances, bending fans' ears with the secrets behind the series. At the same time, though, Mignola avoids message boards, and instead has watched a healthy fan community spring up and become tightly connected around an official website and message board, on hellboy.com. A balance of availability and aloofness has made Mignola a unique figure among readers, allowing them to connect to the work through brief interactions with the artist himself and through the behind-the-scenes information in his books, while nurturing their own rich community of fandom and preserving the mystery.

Another factor in the appeal of the Hellboy stories is the order in which they're told. Mignola purposely begins the story of Hellboy fifty years after Hellboy's appearance on earth. Successive stories jump around in time: shorter stories reveal some of his activities during those missing years, while the longer stories detail his activities in the present day. This flexibility contributes to Hellboy's mythic persona: although decades come and go, Hellboy and his role as a protector of humanity remain fundamentally unchanged.

But the most compelling reason for *Hellboy's* success is that Mike Mignola has created a story that can be read on multiple levels: not only do most readers enjoy the ongoing plot (which spans several centuries and involves a revolving cast of characters), but many are also attracted to the mythic motifs in Hellboy's journey, which you'll see explored further in this book.

DEVELOPMENT

A lthough Mike Mignola was a recognized professional artist before *Hellboy*, working for both DC Comics and Marvel, *Hellboy* represents a breakthrough in Mignola's artistic development. Visually, *Hellboy* is far from the stock interpretations of both horror and hero images. Mignola continues to expand his repertoire as his artwork evolves. *Hellboy's* world has grown from predominantly representational art to an artistic mix sometimes reminiscent of classic illustrators, and other times of abstract backgrounds coupled with iconic figures, designed to resonate subconsciously with readers.

As a writer, Mignola has come full circle. In the early 1990s, he approached the writing aspect of cartooning with hesitation: he plotted but did not script the first Hellboy story. Fifteen years later, he supervises and writes stories of the Hellboy world for others to draw. He is also a patient storyteller: a story appearing in 2005 was first conceived of a decade earlier, but it took ten years to lay the proper groundwork. Mignola's patience as a storyteller is one of his greatest strengths: the power and dynamism of even minor characters in the *Hellboy* saga are products of the care with which Mignola allows characters' stories to evolve over time as he gradually develops their human traits, their mythic overtones, and their significance in *Hellboy's* world.

HELLBOY'S SUPPORTING CAST

T he supporting cast of *Hellboy* is an odd mix. The field team for the B.P.R.D. has included Abe Sapien, a fish-man; Liz Sherman, a pyrokinetic; Roger, a medieval homunculus; Johann Kraus, a disembodied medium; Kate Corrigan, a folklorist; and, most recently, Benjamin Daimio, a Marine who briefly died before becoming field commander of the B.P.R.D. The B.P.R.D. agents appear in most of the *Hellboy* graphic novels, and they were interesting enough to warrant a follow-up ongoing series, co-written by Mignola but characterized by the very different sensibilities of writer John Arcudi and artist Guy Davis.

While much of *Hellboy* deliberately echoes the pulp fiction of the 1920s and '30s, the cast includes several allusions to the Marvel comics Mignola grew up reading. Hellboy himself is in part a nod to the Thing, a member of the Fantastic Four. Abe Sapien recalls the Sub-Mariner, fire starter Liz Sherman is the antithesis of the Human Torch, and Lobster Johnson is reminiscent of pulp heroes the Spider and the Shadow. But Mignola's characters are far from derivative: if anything, their recognizable roots ultimately serve to accentuate their originality.

In recent years, Hellboy has inspired a wide range of spinoffs—from comics, to prose novels, to live-action and animated films. In what directions the Hellboy franchise will grow next is anyone's guess, but with a protagonist so flexible, and a world so ripe for exploration, it is inevitable that the Hellboy mythos will continue to branch out in new directions.

Readers everywhere will be waiting.

CHARACTER PROFILES

by Victoria Blake & Rachel Edidin

ABE SAPIEN

B. P.R.D. agent Abe Sapien was discovered in November 1978, when plumbers repairing a broken pipe in St. Trinian's Hospital happened upon a hidden basement room. Once a secret laboratory for the Oannes Society, the room had been sealed for over a hundred years. In the middle of the room, the plumbers found an amphibious man, unconscious but alive, floating in a sealed tank of water. No clue to the man's identity could be found, but a scrap of paper pinned near his tank read, "Icthyo Sapien—April 14, 1865."

The specimen was sent to B.P.R.D. headquarters in Connecticut for study. There, scientists gave him the nickname "Abe Sapien," because the date on the slip of paper was the exact date of President Abraham Lincoln's assassination. The plumbers were paid $25,000 apiece to keep the discovery a secret.

Abe remained unconscious and unresponsive until March 2, 1979. Just before B.P.R.D. scientist Dr. Roddel readied Abe's body for dissection, his colleague Dr. Cobb suggested that they try electrical stimulation for revival. The electroshock worked, but B.P.R.D. scientists kept the now-conscious Abe in the tank for days, continuing to run various tests on him. The amphibious man showed no obvious signs of intelligence and did not seem to be able to communicate. Hellboy, himself a previous subject of B.P.R.D. tests, intervened on Abe's behalf and rescued him from the laboratory.

Abe came out of his tank healthy if disoriented, and quickly responded to human contact, with Hellboy in particular. Despite no memory of a previous life, Abe was soon able to speak fluent English, apparently remembering the language rather than learning it. Though he was able to stay out of water for up to a week at a time, if he did not soak periodically, his skin would become itchy and rough after a day or two. A water tank was installed in his room at headquarters, and later, on field assignments, he would usually sleep in hotel bathtubs. He was also able to stay underwater for long periods of time, a talent that would serve him well in the field.

Hellboy and Liz Sherman were both particularly fond of Abe, and the three of them formed a lasting friendship. Hellboy quickly convinced B.P.R.D. director Trevor Bruttenholm to let Abe come along on minor field operations so that the fish-man could learn about the world outside the Bureau. Between April and June 1979, Abe was Hellboy's constant companion.

Although Abe's existence was never officially top secret, his discovery in that basement was never revealed, and he never became a public figure, whereas Hellboy had grown up in the public eye. Nervous about his appearance, Abe insisted on wearing a simple disguise consisting of a trench coat, a hat, gloves, and sometimes sunglasses and a false beard. Hellboy didn't like disguises, due to his own self-image as a normal working stiff, an average Joe. "Let them stare," he'd say to Abe, "they'll get used to you." But Hellboy had the advantage of a personality that always won him acceptance, despite his appearance. Abe was never comfortable with the attention, which contributed to even some of his fellow agents considering him cold and aloof, if perhaps better mannered than Hellboy. Hellboy's theory for why people have been able to accept a seven-foot-tall red man with horns and a tail more easily than a fish-man was simply that "Everybody's seen the weird stuff that lives in the ocean. They know that stuff is real—it scares them. The whole hell and the devil thing is a bit more abstract."

In June 1979, a romance with archaeologist Anastasia Bransfield drew Hellboy away, leaving Abe largely stranded at B.P.R.D. headquarters. Liz and Abe developed a brother-and-sister relationship based on their mutual "freak" status as wards of the B.P.R.D.; Director Bruttenholm stood in as a father figure, although Abe's

relationship to him was more one of respect and gratitude than actual warmth.

In 1980, Liz was made a full field agent, leaving Abe alone at headquarters as she began to travel on assignment. Abe grew jealous of Liz's freedom—she was able to become a part of the world in ways Abe felt he never would. Still, Liz spent as much time as possible with Abe between missions.

In 1981, although still not an official agent, Abe joined a small group of agents on his first mission without Hellboy— his first mission since Hellboy had left with Bransfield two years earlier. The simple assignment of investigating a wrecked ship off the coast of Spain turned into a disaster, with three agents dead, as well as many civilians. However, Abe proved himself, and, as a result, was made a full field agent that March. Hellboy soon returned to the Bureau, and for the next fourteen years, Hellboy, Liz, and Abe often worked together as a team on assignments.

In May 1994, Abe and Liz joined Hellboy to investigate Trevor Bruttenholm's death. The agents traveled to Cavendish Hall in upstate New York, where the mad monk

Rasputin tried to recruit Hellboy to his cause. Rasputin's larger goal, which he tried to achieve using Liz's pyrokinetic power and the ancient creature Sadu-Hem, was to release the Ogdru Jahad from their prisons to scorch the earth so a new world could rise from the ashes.

While Hellboy confronted Rasputin, Abe was briefly possessed by the spirit of nineteenth-century seaman Elihu Cavendish. In those few moments, Cavendish used Abe to deliver a fatal blow to Rasputin, saving Hellboy, Liz, and possibly the whole world. The experience did nothing to trigger Abe's memory of his previous life, in which he had actually known Cavendish.

Following the incident at Cavendish Hall, Abe and Liz returned to headquarters without Hellboy. Abe tried to help Liz recover from her ordeal with Rasputin, but in the end, the trauma was too much, and she made the decision to quit the B.P.R.D. With Liz gone, Abe focused on his fieldwork with Hellboy.

In February 1997, a team of agents was sent to search for the vampire Vladimir Giurescu, whose body had been stolen from a New York wax museum. The mission took the team to Romania, where Abe and Agent Scott Clark were lured into a trap apparently set by locals loyal to the vampire. Clark died in the trap—he was speared through the chest when the floor of a church collapsed—and Abe broke his arm. In the basement below the church, Abe was confronted by the ghost of Rasputin, who told him that he would be punished for Rasputin's murder, and that he would die as Rasputin had, concluding, "The hands on the spear shaft will belong to another [but] the heart that drives them will be mine." A moment later, the severed head of a local priest told Abe, "Sunken bells are tolling for thee. Out of the caverns of Num-Yabisc, dark and terrible deep, the ocean is calling her children home." Though Abe did not understand this declaration, it filled him with a sense of impending doom.

Upon his rescue by the B.P.R.D. team, Abe learned that his dread was not misplaced. Liz Sherman, who had encountered a homunculus during the mission to Romania, was dying, apparently from losing her fire to the homunculus. Abe stayed with Liz for several days at a Romanian hospital, up to the moment of her death— a much more crushing blow to Abe than Bruttenholm's death a few years earlier. Fortunately, Hellboy found the homunculus and compelled him to return the stolen fire to Liz. The creature, whom Hellboy had named Roger on the way to the hospital, was able to return Liz's power,

bringing the girl instantly back to life, at the expense of his own.

A few months later, back at B.P.R.D. headquarters, scientists Cobb and Roddel prepared to dissect the now-lifeless homunculus Roger in the same way that they had almost dissected Abe. When the scientists stepped out of the laboratory for lunch, Abe rerouted electricity into Roger, causing serious damage to the headquarters' electrical system, but zapping the homunculus back to life and ultimately bringing another major player to the B.P.R.D. team. Abe's sense of doom was beginning to lift.

In May 1999, Abe and Hellboy traveled to Lochmaben, Scotland, to investigate the theft of a box and a set of tongs that had once belonged to Saint Dunstan. Abe was shot and tortured with a hot poker by a monkey. He made a full recovery from his injuries, but his feeling of impending doom had begun to return. However, following the example of Liz Sherman, he put on a brave face and continued to devote himself to his B.P.R.D. duties.

Abe's fears proved justified when Liz once again left the Bureau, this time in order to study at a monastery in the Ural Mountains to try to finally control her power.

Things soon got worse when Hellboy quit the Bureau. Though Abe continued to work as a field agent, he began to feel more and more isolated, and considered leaving the B.P.R.D. himself, although he couldn't imagine where he'd go.

Liz's spirit appeared to Abe in September 2002, pleading with him to help her. Abe, along with new B.P.R.D. agents Johann Kraus and Roger, traveled to the Ural Mountains, where they discovered Liz's lifeless body within the ravaged monastery. Abe stepped up as the team's leader as they descended into the earth and rescued Liz Sherman's spirit from a primitive race who'd captured it to somehow power their machines. Afterward, Liz decided to return to the Bureau, and a new spirit of teamwork developed among the crew, with Abe and Liz's brother-sister team as its foundation. For the following two years, they worked together in investigations around the globe.

One night in July 2004, Abe dreamt of dead bodies falling into an undersea pit. In the background of the dream, he once again heard the voice of the decapitated Romanian priest telling him that "sunken bells are tolling for thee," and that the ocean was "calling her children home."

At the same time, a strange fungal version of the Sadu-Hem creature, which had been discovered as a spore in a routine investigation of the ruins of Cavendish Hall, escaped from the B.P.R.D. laboratory in New Jersey. The B.P.R.D. team tracked the fungus to Crab Point, Michigan, where Humbert T. Jones, the West Virginia Miracle Boy, led a congregation of townspeople transformed into frog creatures. Inside Jones's house, Abe discovered a shrine to Rasputin. A moment later, Abe was impaled by Jones, fulfilling the prophecy that he would die as Rasputin had died: "The hands on the spear shaft will belong to another [but] the heart that drives them will be mine."

At the moment of Abe's death, his spirit traveled back in time to an ancient undersea temple where he saw a mysterious alien sea creature. Watching as centuries passed, Abe saw the temple fall into ruins, and observed the alien creature curling in on itself and becoming something resembling an egg. Abe then saw a man in a diving suit remove the egg from the temple and return to a submarine. As if in a dream, Abe found himself walking the halls of St. Trinian's Hospital in Washington in 1865. Outside, it

rained frogs as Abe entered the secret Oannes Society laboratory in the basement of the hospital. Inside, Langdon Everett Caul and other Society members tried to communicate with the egglike entity. Abe was invisible to everybody in the room except for Caul, and was suddenly drawn into Caul's body, becoming a part of him. Caul fell into a coma, and the other Society members placed his body in a tube, and observed the beginning of his transformation, before sealing him in that same basement where he'd be discovered a century later by the plumbers repairing a pipe. Apparently, Abe's spirit had gone back in time, joining Caul to create himself.

Though he had lost a lot of blood and had been declared dead by B.P.R.D. medics in Crab Point, Abe suddenly returned to life. Despite having been speared through the chest, Abe made a surprisingly fast recovery in the days and weeks that followed.

The trip back in time did not bring back any of Abe's memories of his previous life, but it did give him a name: Langdon Everett Caul. Abe knew intuitively that his near-death experience had been more than a dream, and, compelled to discover the central mystery of his life, he began to research Caul. This led him to Littleport, Rhode Island, where Caul had lived with his wife, Edith Howard. She'd killed herself when Caul had disappeared in 1865. At Caul's dilapidated house, Edith's ghost appeared to Abe and tried to persuade him to remain with her in a dream-world recreation of their old life. Though he was tempted—Abe had never dreamt

of being a normal man or having a wife, and it was a profound experience for him—he ultimately decided that he could not live in a dream, however appealing. Telling Edith that he belonged in the real world, however difficult living in that world might be, Abe helped her to face her own death—freeing her to continue on to whatever afterlife awaited her.

Abe returned to the B.P.R.D.'s new Colorado headquarters more haunted and distant than ever, sharing only a few details of his experience—and those only with Kate Corrigan, who'd gone with him to Rhode Island. But even she wasn't privy to his thoughts about what he'd experienced, and his behavior grew erratic. He withdrew from his friends and coworkers—including new team leader Benjamin Daimio—but made strange attempts to act more like the man he once was, including trying to wear conventional clothing over his very unconventional body. His speech patterns changed, in an either deliberate or subconscious attempt to sound like a man of a hundred years ago—a man he still couldn't remember, and only knew from the bits and pieces he learned in his strange investigations.

Preoccupied with his recent discoveries, Abe stepped away from his duties at the Bureau as it faced a grave new threat in the form of a plague of frogs—a growing population of frog creatures spreading across the northern United States. Abe

and the rest of the team were dealt a terrible blow when Roger the Homunculus was killed in action. Abe blamed himself and his retreat from fieldwork for Roger's death, and overcompensated by rushing off into battle and nearly getting himself killed. The frogs ultimately retreated underground—cold comfort for the team, which spent the next few months trying to find a way to revive Roger, to no avail. Abe continued to wrestle with the ghosts of his past, including Langdon Everett Caul—trying to figure out who he should be.

In early 2007, a further clue came in the form of a cigar box with the initials L.E.C. engraved upon it. Abe went halfway around the world looking for answers— to Indonesia, where he was confronted by bizarre figures from his previous life: his fellow members of the Oannes Society, who now occupied crude cybernetic bodies of Victorian-era design, and plotted to reunite mankind with divinity by killing millions of people. In their company, Abe learned more of his lost past and recognized that the man he once had been had precious little in common with the man he had since become. Finally, he foiled his former comrades' plans and returned to his true home and family: the B.P.R.D.

AMELIA DUNN

Amelia Dunn was born June 3, 1857, in Providence, Rhode Island. An only child, Miss Dunn never married, and led an uneventful life until her mid-forties, when, in the summer of 1902, her parents were discovered murdered in their home. Because she still lived with her parents, Miss Dunn was suspected in the murders, and the local papers referred to her as the Rhode Island Lizzie Borden until investigators finally determined that Mr. Dunn had murdered his wife and then killed himself. After the death of her parents, Miss Dunn became deeply involved in spiritualism, conducting séances in her home.

In 1911, Miss Dunn contacted a spirit identifying himself simply as William. William claimed to have been a member of the highest order of the Heliopic Brotherhood of Ra, and to have learned to mentally project himself back in time. Over the course of many years of doing this, William had recorded "the true Secret History of the World." However, he told Miss Dunn that he had died in 1892, and that all his notes had been destroyed. Over the next two years, William dictated the Secret History to her.

The rest of Miss Dunn's life was consumed with trying to get the Secret History published. At first, she tried to attract the attention of major publishers, but after a few years, she eventually turned to smaller presses. Several expressed interest, but extenuating circumstances repeatedly prevented publication. The first publisher to agree to release the book, Buckminster, Ltd., claimed that a sudden strike at a binding shop required them to cancel publication. Miss Dunn accepted an offer from Root & Standish; however, years of bad management forced them to close their doors before they could publish the book. Around this time, the Dunn home began to be plagued by poltergeist activity, which Amelia attributed to William and other spirits, who were frustrated at her inability to get the book published.

Miss Dunn spent the rest of her inheritance in an attempt to self-publish the Secret History. The book was printed, but a warehouse fire destroyed the small print run. The original manuscript may also have been destroyed, as it has never been located.

By this time, Miss Dunn was a broken woman and never again left her home. The poltergeist activity had by this time apparently ended, and she never reported hearing from William again, although toward the end she did claim to be visited by the ghosts of her parents. She died in her parents' bed on September 13, 1928. To the end, she believed herself the victim of a great conspiracy by "governments and the giants of industry," who sought to keep the "great truths" from the common man.

BABA YAGA

The Baba Yaga, a Slavic ogress and witch, flies by night in a wooden mortar, steering with a pestle and churning up storms in her wake. Her name has been used for centuries to scare disrespectful children into obedience. A fearsome crone with iron teeth and wooden legs, she lives in a house set atop a giant chicken leg, with a wooden fence decorated with the skulls and bones of the children she's devoured. Though most legends portray her as a vicious cannibal, she's sometimes worshiped as a woodland goddess, guarding the fountains and waters of life, controlling inspiration and creativity.

In 1895, she appeared to the twenty-six-year-old Grigori Yefimovich Rasputin in a vision, telling him that the fates had chosen him as their "agent of change, father of a new millennium." In 1900, she visited Rasputin again, this time in the flesh. Rasputin gave her one-half of his soul to hide in the roots of the World Tree so that, whatever happened to him, his spirit could "live forever in the heart of the world."

In March 1964, while investigating the disappearance of several children near the village of Bereznik, Russia, Hellboy encountered the Baba Yaga in a cemetery where she was counting the fingers of dead sinners. During the ensuing fight, he accidentally shot out her left eye. She escaped, but apparently punished the nearby village—spring did not come to Bereznik. Winter lasted all year, and every child born in the village that year was born blind in one eye.

The Baba Yaga's injury was so terrible that she retreated to the World Tree to recuperate, and, according to her servant Koku, "She is faded out of the world." She dwells now "beyond the thrice-nine lands, in the thrice-tenth kingdom."

In 1997, she sent Koku to deliver an iron maiden to Rasputin, whose spirit form continued to walk the earth. Whether it was intended to help him or not is unclear. The iron maiden originally had belonged to Elizabeth Bathory, the Hungarian Blood Countess. Rasputin used it to transform Ilsa Haupstein, intending to create a replacement for Hellboy, but instead providing a vessel for the displaced spirit of Hecate.

Regardless of her motives, the Baba Yaga continued to show an interest in Rasputin. After the destruction of Rasputin's spirit in a confrontation with Hecate in 2001, the Baba Yaga rescued what was left of him, and placed it in an acorn, which she hung around her neck, "close to [her] heart forever."

Forever didn't last long. In 2007, after Hellboy had turned down the witches' request that he lead them, the Baba Yaga's servant Koku convinced the witches to give Hellboy to his mistress. The Baba Yaga called upon the immortal warrior Koshchei the Deathless to serve as her champion, and over the course of his battle with Hellboy, the Baba Yaga imbued Koshchei with all of her power—even intending to use the final bit of Rasputin that until then she had kept faithfully in the acorn. However, her servant Koku took the acorn from the Baba Yaga before she could use it, and dropped it among the roots of the World Tree, where it was lost. Ultimately, the Baba Yaga was unable to defeat Hellboy, and the ancient witch was left a drained husk of her former self.

BENJAMIN DAIMIO

Benjamin Daimio was born on May 26, 1970, in Poquoson, Virginia, to a mixed Japanese-American family. At the time of his birth, Daimio's father served as a U.S. Air Force pilot in Vietnam. His father's name was Masaru, but he insisted on being called Max. Ben was named after Benjamin Franklin and was raised 100 percent American, with no connection to Japanese culture or history.

Daimio's father remained in the Air Force after the American withdrawal from Vietnam. His parents divorced when he was twelve, and Daimio lived with his mother, first in Virginia, then in New Jersey. When Daimio turned eighteen, he joined the Marines, embracing any opportunity that would put him in the heart of action. Thriving within the strictly regimented structure of military life, he rose through the hierarchy and was promoted to the rank of captain during Desert Storm.

In the spring of 2001, Captain Daimio led a platoon of eight American Marines into the jungles of Bolivia to rescue a group of nuns thought to have been kidnapped by a political group, the True Path. The platoon was attacked by a group of locals who appeared to be part of a primitive Jaguar Cult. The Marines killed the natives,

but were set upon by a gigantic creature, which was obscured by the shadows and the jungle. During the fight, Daimio was attacked by the animated corpse of one of the nuns. The nun-zombie, likely an extension of the larger creature, bit Daimio and ripped the flesh off his face. The large creature suddenly appeared to Daimio as the jaguar god, telling him, "The old world is your soul . . . the new world is life." The last thing Daimio saw before he died was the jaguar god's gaping mouth. Three days later, on June 13, Daimio came back to life in a military morgue.

Daimio joined the B.P.R.D. as field commander in 2004, during the Bureau's relocation to an abandoned base in the Colorado mountains. Daimio brought his military experience to the position, requiring B.P.R.D. agents to work within a rigid chain of command. Though some agents chafed at the change—none more so than Liz Sherman, who'd grown up at the B.P.R.D.—Roger the Homunculus took to it

immediately. Over a series of missions attempting to eradicate the growing number of frog creatures, Roger began to emulate Daimio's militaristic attitude.

In 2005, Roger was killed during a sweep of a frog-creature nest, which led to a confrontation with the Black Flame. Guilt over Roger's death weighed on Daimio, causing him to ease his rigid military discipline. The apparent end to the frog threat also contributed to his more casual attitude.

Since the encounter with the Black Flame, Daimio had been plagued by strange nightmares and a mysterious affliction, leading him to seek the aid of a Wu—a Chinese master of mystical physiology.

In late 2006, Daimio accompanied agent Abe Sapien to Indonesia on a mission where the two foiled a plot to kill millions, marking a kind of return to duty for Abe. The mission also brought about a new level of cooperation between the two, who worked not as commander and subordinate agent, but as equals.

Daimio's camaraderie with his colleagues—and his status as their commander—were both to be short-lived. In 2007, the secret of Daimio's resurrection reared its head: the jaguar god had returned Daimio to life, but in the process, the captain had become an "emissary of the jaguar god," half-human, half-demon. He had been able to keep the jaguar god's influence at bay with the aid of the Wu, but it eventually grew too powerful for Daimio to resist. He transformed into a powerful and bloodthirsty human/jaguar hybrid and killed several B.P.R.D. agents—as well as the Wu and Johann Kraus's new body—before fleeing into the Colorado mountains. Thus far, the B.P.R.D. has been unable to locate Daimio, or to ascertain whether his condition is reversible.

EDWARD GREY

E dward Grey[1] was born September 16, 1856, in West Sussex, England. His mother died when he was only three years old, and he spent his childhood on the 172-acre estate of Lord Robert Hastings, where his father worked as game warden. His formal schooling was brief—he spent only four years at a country school. Most of his time was spent out of doors, and his education came from hunters and other country people, and the ghost stories and weird fairy tales they told him.

When the boy was twelve, a number of cows from Lord Robert Hastings's herd were found slaughtered in the woods. Three children disappeared soon after, and the local men formed search parties. Grey, who suspected the real nature of the killer, tracked the predator to its lair in the Hastings family vault. The creature was one of Hastings's sons, recently returned from school in Paris. Apparently he had contracted the werewolf curse there, and since his return home he had been secretly devouring the corpses in the family vault. However, those could not satisfy him for long, and, unable to control himself, he had ventured out, killing cattle and children. Although Grey was badly injured in the fight, he finally killed the werewolf with a bullet blessed by a local priest.

Lord Hastings never attempted to conceal what his son had done. He worked with the local priest to see that the boy's body was burned and the ashes scattered. He repaid his debt to Grey by inviting the boy to recuperate in the estate house, and providing him with the best medical attention, as well as the attention of the priest, to make sure the boy would not inherit the werewolf curse. During his long recovery, Grey developed a genuine affection for his benefactor. He was impressed by the honesty and compassion with which Lord Hastings dealt with the aftermath of the werewolf attacks, specifically what he had done for the families of the slain

---

[1] Not to be confused with Edward Grey, First Viscount Grey of Fallodon, 1862–1933.

children. His example would stay with Grey throughout his life as the standard for true nobility and honor in times of crisis. Hastings, in turn, grew very fond of the young Grey, preferring the boy to his own sons, all of whom had been changed for the worse by their city education. Lord Hastings preferred life in the country, and the people he found there. He arranged for Grey to get a good education, but kept him on the estate, so he wouldn't be ruined by boarding schools or universities as had Hastings's own children, who now squandered the family fortune on lives of leisure and vice. Grey became a minor celebrity in West Sussex. There were many tales of his encounters with supernatural creatures, although how many of these are factual and how many are regional folklore is impossible to determine.

In 1876, associates of Lord Hastings sent news of a haunting in the Tower of London, and Hastings recommended Grey, then twenty years old, to investigate the matter. Grey traveled to London, where he confronted a bearlike creature believed to be the ghost of Lord Jeffreys, the hanging judge of the Monmouth Rebellion (1685), who drank himself to death in the tower. It's uncertain how Grey dealt with the creature, but there were no further disturbances.

City life was exciting, and even in London, Grey was seen as a larger-than-life character. He quickly became a darling of the media and the aristocracy, who dogged his heels and threw grand parties in his honor. However, Grey longed for the outdoors and the country. As soon as the tower incident was behind him, he began making plans to leave the city. He'd attracted royal attention, though, and Prime Minister Benjamin Disraeli visited him on behalf of Queen Victoria. The queen wanted Grey to stay on as a special agent to the crown, dealing with occult matters. The Heliopic Brotherhood of Ra was in its heyday, and Victoria and Disraeli worried that the H.B.R. planned to interfere with Britain's own imperial agenda. Grey couldn't refuse his queen, and grew accustomed to city life while operating in secret for the crown.

In February 1879, Grey foiled a plot by a coven of witches to murder the queen. He had stopped them just in time, and the next month was knighted for "special services in the protection of Crown and Country." Most of what Sir Edward Grey did for the government remains unknown, still considered top-secret information over a hundred years later. What little we know about his exploits come from the few journals and letters that researchers have uncovered over the years.

In August 1882, Grey apparently uncovered a plot by the visiting nobleman vampire Vladimir Giurescu to establish a "secret evil empire" in England. Grey wounded the creature and forced him to flee back to Romania. The Dutch warlock Epke Vrooman wasn't so lucky. In 1884, Grey discovered him living in London under an assumed name. Vrooman fled by boat, but Grey pursued him, finally killing him near the French island of Saint-Sébastien.

From 1884 to 1889, Sir Edward Grey focused his attention on the increasingly bizarre activities of the Heliopic Brotherhood of Ra and its chartered branches, the Knights of the Silver Star and the Knights of Abydos. In 1888, Grey aided in the investigation of the Jack the Ripper killings, but his exact role in the case remains a mystery. A few months later, Grey had a falling-out with Queen Victoria, and it was rumored to be over the government's decision to suppress the Ripper's true identity. In February 1889, Grey left government service, but, a loyal subject of the crown, he never revealed any classified information, including what he knew about the Ripper case.

Grey established an independent "occult detective" practice in Whitechapel—the same slum where the Ripper killings had occurred. As a private detective, he maintained the same secrecy and discretion he'd developed during his years of government service, but in other ways he was a changed man. He'd previously maintained secrecy despite a colorful personality and bombastic style—a drinker and a brawler, still a country boy at heart. His falling-out with the queen left him much more reserved, grim, and solitary. Both his father and Lord Hastings had died years earlier, and though Grey had inherited a substantial amount of money from the Hastings estate, he chose to continue living in relative poverty.

Grey worked as an occult detective in London from February 1889 to July 1908. The details of most of his cases remain unknown even to authorities, but it was Grey who turned the notorious witch Abigail Wodehouse over to Scotland Yard in 1892. He monitored the Heliopic Brotherhood of Ra closely before the closing of the Universal Temple in September 1893, and evidence suggests that he tracked their activities as they continued as an underground society.

Into the twentieth century, Grey investigated the increasingly strange rumors of the Heliopic Brotherhood's activities in Europe. Upon learning of the June 30, 1908, explosion in the Tunguska Forest in Siberia—rumored to have been caused by an H.B.R. ceremony—Grey closed his London office and a short time later left England for the Continent. Nothing is known of his activities there, or the extent of his travels for the next six years.

Grey resurfaced in New York City on April 13, 1914. He appeared less grim than he had during his later years in London and his name appeared often in the society pages of the *New York Times* and the *New York Sun*. He crossed paths with Houdini several times, and became a frequent guest of the "Boy Mayor," thirty-five-year-old John Purroy Mitchel. Grey once again opened a practice as a private occult detective, and received public attention when he chased a "curious, amphibious, horselike creature" all the way from the Central Park Lake at the Bethesda Terrace into the Hudson.

In late February 1916, Grey heard rumors that the Knights of the Silver Star, a branch of the H.B.R., were holding meetings in Chicago. He left New York by train, arriving in Chicago on March 3. He checked into the Hermitage Hotel at roughly 6:00 p.m., and left an hour later, but did not return.

When concerned friends opened his New York apartment weeks later, they found no personal papers or journals. The great quantity of ash in the fireplace suggested that hundreds of pages had been burned. Either Grey had destroyed his own papers before leaving New York, or someone else had done so after his departure.

Sir Edward Grey was never seen nor heard from again.

ELIHU CAVENDISH AND THE CAVENDISH FAMILY

British sailor and adventurer Elihu Cavendish was born in Suffolk, England, in 1779, the seventh child of Emma and James Cavendish. Growing up under the rough and often violent eye of his father, a blacksmith, Cavendish ran away from home when he was ten, stowing away on a local ship bound for eastern fishing grounds. The captain discovered the boy after a full day of sailing, too late to turn back to port. After a sound beating, Cavendish was allowed to stay on, and the wild stories he heard from the older sailors fired his imagination, cementing his love of the sea and more than making up for the captain's harsh treatment.

When he was fourteen years old, Cavendish signed on as a deckhand on a whaling ship headed for the north Atlantic. He spent the next two years sailing around the world, witnessing strange sights: later, he told friends tales of dead men working in the cane fields of the West Indies; a witch doctor torn to pieces by invisible demons in Madagascar. During this time, rumors spread regarding Cavendish's peculiar habit of disappearing—sometimes for days at a time—in the worst port towns, places "where no sane white man would dare set foot."

While Cavendish's fearlessness earned him the respect of his crewmates, his skill as a whale spotter caught the eyes of the captains under whom he worked. Cavendish quickly rose through the ranks, becoming captain of the *Lydgate* at the unusually young age of twenty-seven.

As a captain, Cavendish saw more than his share of good luck, filling his hold in record time, and on at least two occasions surviving storms that had easily wrecked other ships. His more superstitious sailors whispered that Cavendish's luck stemmed from "unholy pacts with strange dark gods," but most regarded the captain as a good whaler and a stern but fair master.

Whether his fortune was the product of skill, black magic, or divine grace, Cavendish was quickly able to amass a small fortune and purchase five ships. With a fleet of his own, Cavendish decided that it was time to retire from his life at sea and settle down. He purchased a house in Whitby, and in 1809 married a local girl. But Cavendish's luck seemed tied to the sea, and his life at Whitby was plagued with a series of tragedies. Cavendish's bride died in childbirth, followed quickly by his newborn son. The same winter, two of his ships were lost at sea.

Grief stricken, Cavendish swore never to marry again. Abandoning his home in Whitby, he returned to the sea, captaining one of his own ships around the world as distraction from his sorrow. His luck returned, but Cavendish himself had become more grim and silent, and remained further aloof from his men. New rumors arose, of strange doings in foreign ports.

In 1817, during a supply stop in New York, Cavendish took on a new deckhand, a young sailor named Langdon Everett Caul. Cavendish took an immediate liking to young Caul, who seemed more intelligent than most common sailors, and was neither superstitious nor overly religious. Caul was quickly promoted from deckhand to Cavendish's private secretary. Little by little, over the next sixteen years, Cavendish—usually while drinking—told Caul about his adventures and the strange things he had seen.

One night, while particularly drunk, Cavendish told Caul more than usual. Rambling almost incoherently, the captain showed Caul the charms and talismans he had collected from around the world. Finally, he showed Caul his prize possession and closest-guarded secret: a parchment covered in strange symbols, which Cavendish believed spoke of a great secret buried somewhere in the Arctic.

The next day, when Cavendish sobered up, he regretted having revealed so much. In the weeks and months that followed, Cavendish became more and more paranoid and distrustful of Caul, until June 1833, when Caul finally left the ship and Cavendish's command.

By 1836, Cavendish had built his fleet to twelve ships, all with trustworthy and competent captains capable of operating independently. Finally, Cavendish was free to sail to the Arctic to pursue the great secret he believed awaited him there.

The following year, Cavendish set off on his first Arctic expedition. With his best ship and a handpicked crew, he sailed north through English waters and past Norway, where his famous luck finally ran out. His ship was trapped in the pack ice in Baffin Bay, west of Greenland. The six-month struggle back to civilization cost the lives of half Cavendish's crew and left him physically and emotionally shattered.

While recovering at a hospital in Bath, England, Cavendish met and became deeply attached to a nurse named Betty Hathaway, whom he married after a perfunctory courtship.

During the escape from his doomed ship, Cavendish had grown close to a Native American harpooner, who had lost a hand to frostbite. Upon their return to England, the harpooner became Cavendish's personal servant and constant companion. The many Indian legends of North America he told Cavendish piqued the captain's interest in the continent, and in 1841, when Cavendish was well enough to leave the hospital, Cavendish, his new wife, and the harpooner set sail for New York.

They settled on a tiny island in the middle of Lake Talutah, in upstate New York. Although the island was shunned by local Indian tribes, the harpooner convinced Cavendish that it was a place of powerful magic, where Cavendish would recover his strength. There, Cavendish oversaw the construction of Cavendish Hall, which would serve as the seat of the Cavendish family for many generations to come. He knew nothing of what lay beneath his new home—a massive underground temple where the Ogdru Jahad had been worshiped seven centuries before.

Even while he was recovering, building his home, and establishing his new family, Cavendish continued to plan for his next expedition to the Arctic. But he never regained his former strength. In the summer of 1847, only months before Cavendish was to undertake his second voyage north, he contracted typhus and died, leaving behind his wife and their three young sons.

Cavendish's quest for the Arctic did not end with his death. Like a curse, the obsession passed down from generation to generation of his family. Every male descendent of Elihu Cavendish tried to reach the Arctic, and each of the expeditions met with failure—many ended in death. With each successive generation, the family's reputation as intrepid and sometimes foolhardy explorers grew as their fortune diminished.

Early in 1992, when the last of the Cavendish sons—William, James, and Henry—were planning for their own Arctic expedition, they were contacted by B.P.R.D. founder Trevor Bruttenholm through a series of mutual friends. Bruttenholm had been conducting his own Arctic research and believed that he could decipher a good deal of the ancient language on Elihu Cavendish's treasured parchment, which had inspired the family's doomed expeditions for over a century.

In November 1992, the Cavendish brothers, Bruttenholm, and Swedish mountaineer Sven Olafsen left New York for Bull Harbor, which was to be the jumping-off point for the journey north. Because of Bruttenholm's translations, the 1992 expedition was ultimately able to discover what no other Cavendishes had—the remains of a Hyperborean temple in the Arctic. Inside the temple, they discovered the secret that was hinted at on the parchment: the ancient creature Sadu-Hem, one of the 369 Ogdru Hem, "left by the Ogdru Jahad that they might always have a foothold in this world."

Unfortunately, the group also discovered Sadu-Hem's acolyte, Rasputin. The Cavendish brothers and Olafsen were transformed into amphibious creatures; Bruttenholm alone was allowed to escape unchanged, although the details of the encounter were never revealed.

The Cavendish brothers, now frog creatures, returned to Cavendish Hall. Two of the transformed brothers killed their mother, who had been waiting for their return. One of the frog creatures tracked down and killed Bruttenholm, and was subsequently destroyed by Hellboy.

While investigating the strange events at Cavendish Hall, Abe Sapien discovered the preserved body of Elihu Cavendish and was briefly possessed by his spirit long enough to hurl a harpoon into Rasputin. The blow destroyed Rasputin's physical form, and stopped him from releasing the Ogdru Jahad from their prisons. Moments later, a massive explosion destroyed Cavendish Hall. The last remaining members of the Cavendish line—the two brothers, now frog creatures—lived beneath the ruins until their deaths in a routine reconnaissance mission by B.P.R.D. agents in 2005.

ELIZABETH SHERMAN

Elizabeth Anne Sherman was born in Kansas City, Kansas, on April 15, 1962. She was raised in a strictly religious family and attended Catholic school as well as twice-weekly Mass.

Liz's pyrokinetic ability first manifested itself when she was ten. Small fires—no bigger than a match head—began to flare up near her. She kept the fires a secret, extinguishing them before they could spread. However, as time passed, the fires began to appear more frequently—by February 1973, they were a daily occurrence. Liz was convinced that the fires were her fault—punishment for some unknown sin—and she turned more and more to prayer as a means of managing her guilt.

For a time, prayer seemed to work: by April, the fires had stopped completely, probably controlled by Liz's will and determination.

In July 1973, Liz thought she had her problem under control. However, a neighborhood boy made fun of Liz's ponytail, and her anger manifested in a fire that leveled an entire city block and killed thirty-two people, including Liz's parents and younger brother. Firefighters discovered Liz, miraculously unharmed, standing in the middle of the smoldering rubble.

The B.P.R.D., which had been called to the scene, wanted to take custody of Liz immediately, but the request was blocked by Liz's family, who refused to believe investigators' claims—or Liz's—that she had been responsible for the fire. They soon learned otherwise, as small fires once again began to flare up around her. Over the next ten months, Liz grew increasingly depressed as she was passed from relative to relative—her extended family was understandably afraid of her destructive powers—until she finally became a ward of the B.P.R.D. in May 1974.

At B.P.R.D. headquarters, Liz was kept in a flame-proof room while the Bureau scientists studied her power. With no real comfort or physical contact—only doctors and scientists in bulky flame-proof suits were allowed to enter her room—Liz withdrew further and further into depression.

Her isolation was finally broken by Hellboy, who became her closest friend and source of "human" contact in those first weeks. Hellboy helped Liz to overcome her trauma, fear, and isolation, and to adjust to her new home in the B.P.R.D. For the

next six years, Liz and Hellboy remained extremely close—he traveled frequently on assignments, but made sure to check in on Liz regularly—as she trained with both the B.P.R.D. scientists and independent experts on pyrokinesis, developing at least tenuous control of her abilities.

In 1978, Abe Sapien was brought to B.P.R.D. headquarters. Much like Liz, Abe was held in a tank while scientists studied him. Like Liz, Abe was rescued from his confinement by Hellboy, with whom he developed a deep and lasting friendship. When Hellboy was away from Bureau headquarters, Abe and Liz, too, became fast friends independent of their mutual savior. While Liz still occasionally had nightmares about the fire that had killed her family, she gradually began to let go of her past life. And while she was still far from complete control of her powers, the number of accidental flare-ups continued to steadily decrease.

In 1980, when Liz reached legal adulthood, she decided to remain with the B.P.R.D., which had offered her a position as a full field agent. In the field, Liz continued to struggle with her pyrokinetic abilities. In stressful situations, she often lost control of her power, and, as a result, she was often assigned to quieter cases. Between 1980 and 1994, she quit the B.P.R.D. twelve times, though she always returned—no matter how much she wanted to leave the Bureau, she didn't trust herself in the outside world.

In May 1994, Abe, Liz, and Hellboy traveled to Cavendish Hall in upstate New York to investigate the murder of B.P.R.D. director Trevor Bruttenholm. During the course of the investigation, Rasputin seized control of Liz's power, funneling it through the creature Sadu-Hem and "into the void," where he hoped it would free the Ogdru Jahad from their prison. Rasputin might have succeeded in his mission had Abe not killed him, spearing him through the chest with a whaling harpoon. Liz, shocked out of her trancelike state when Rasputin died, was unable to regain control of her fire. In the explosion that followed, she destroyed both Sadu-Hem and Cavendish Hall.

Liz was devastated by both the violation of being used by Rasputin and her own loss of control, and she quit the B.P.R.D. for the thirteenth time in June 1994. But if Liz did not trust her power within the B.P.R.D., she was even less confident of her control in the outside world; she returned to the Bureau the following February.

In 1997, Liz joined agents Bud Waller and Sidney Leach on a search for the body of the vampire Vladimir Giurescu. In the course of their investigation, the group discovered the seemingly lifeless body of a man-sized homunculus in a castle in Romania. Liz was drawn to the homunculus and, sensing a way to be rid of her fire, she put her finger into a hole in the homunculus's chest. Her fire drained into the homunculus, bringing it to life. When Waller shot Liz in the arm in an attempt to break the connection, the homunculus killed him, then fled.

The price of the exchange had been steeper than Liz could have anticipated: her fire was integral to her life, and without it, she wasted away and died in a Romanian hospital. She was only dead a few minutes, however, before the homunculus—which Hellboy had named Roger—restored her to life by returning her stolen fire to her.

Liz returned to work, but death had taken a psychic toll on her. In February 2000, she left the B.P.R.D. once again, this time traveling to a monastery in the Ural Mountains, where she hoped to be able to achieve some semblance of balance and make peace with her fire.

Although Liz never discussed the details of her experience at the monastery, by mid-2002, she had finally achieved the equilibrium she sought—and with it, full control of her powers. Unfortunately, in September 2002, the monastery was attacked

by descendents of a Hyperborean slave race, which had been living deep in the earth. All of the monks were murdered in the attack. Liz's spirit was stolen out of her body and imprisoned inside a Hyperborean device that the King of Fear, the leader of the slaves, planned to use to power ancient war machines. Liz was somehow able to broadcast her distress to Abe, who mobilized a B.P.R.D. rescue mission. Liz was rescued, and her spirit was restored to her body. Though shaken by her experience, Liz retained her newfound balance and was soon traveling with the B.P.R.D. on other assignments.

One such mission involved a spore that B.P.R.D. scientists had discovered during a routine sweep of Cavendish Hall. The spore had grown into an earthly manifestation of Sadu-Hem, which had escaped from the B.P.R.D. laboratory and traveled to Crab Point, Michigan, where it transformed the town's entire population into frog creatures. During that investigation, Liz was able to control her fire, using it to destroy both Sadu-Hem (again) and an enclave of frog creatures.

Despite Liz's efforts, some of the frog creatures escaped. Liz, along with other B.P.R.D. agents, traveled all over the country trying to eradicate the frog creatures. After the B.P.R.D. had destroyed a nest in Handelson, Montana, an old woman approached Liz and gave her a lotus blossom, which apparently caused Liz to lapse into a brief coma. While she was unconscious, Liz dreamt of a mysterious gentleman who seemed to know things about the frog creatures. With his guidance, she was able to channel her power through an ancient Hyperborean artifact, and destroy the enormous creature Katha-Hem, one of the Ogdru Hem summoned by the frog creatures. She was not, however, able to save Roger from being destroyed by a former C.E.O. of the Zinco Corporation, who

had adopted the identity of the Black Flame in homage to the World War II Nazi villain of the same name.

Feeling responsible for Roger's death, Liz moved into his old room to be closer to his things. In 2007, her mistrust of new B.P.R.D. field leader Benjamin Daimio proved sound when Daimio transformed into a jaguar creature, killing several operatives and attacking Liz. The mysterious gentleman was able to use this incident to extend his influence over Liz, when she once again lapsed into a coma. She was awakened when Johann, possessed by the spirit of Lobster Johnson, appeared and shot the stranger.

Liz's visions persist, with increasingly apocalyptic imagery, and the mysterious gentleman's warnings grow more grave, along with his promise that he alone can help her stop what's coming. The identity and intent of her visitor remains a mystery, as does the true nature of his interest in Liz.

THE FAIRIES

There are many theories about the origins of fairies. Some believe them to be the spirits of the ancient dead, souls not bad enough to be sent to hell, but not good enough to earn a place in heaven. Others link them to the original fallen angels, who weren't thrown down to hell with Satan, but only fell as far as earth—some into caverns just below the earth, some into the sea, and still others into the forests and fields. Many beliefs about fairies predate Christendom, and some see the fairies as the old gods themselves, nature spirits once worshiped but now mostly forgotten, their influence gradually fading out of the world.

Whatever their origins, there are hundreds of different kinds of fairies—gnomes, elves, goblins, pixies, mermaids, trolls, kobolds, knockers, and selkies. Some are clearly evil, while others bring good fortune. However, most are unpredictable—sometimes helpful, rewarding humans for some good service, but more often mischievous or outright harmful. They're known to lead travelers astray, and there are many stories of fairies stealing human children to raise as their own. Fairies are quick to anger if they feel they've been slighted, and are known to hold long grudges.

In the last hundred years, fairy sightings have become very rare. It's suspected that most have died, or abandoned the world. There are still scattered bands, sometimes called trooping fairies, like the group of trolls that killed several people in Norway in 1962; or solitary creatures haunting out-of-the-way places, like the old border goblin, Iron Shoes, who was destroyed in 1961—but such sightings have all but ended over the last fifty years.

Fairies have been seen in one form or another all over the world, but Hellboy's most significant interactions have been with the Irish fairies, the Daoine Sídhe, or the Tuatha Dé Danann.

In 1959, Hellboy visited an Irish family by the name of Monaghan whose baby Alice was acting strangely. Hellboy discovered that the baby was actually a changeling and, using iron tongs (iron being poisonous to most fairies), forced it to give him information leading to the recovery of the baby.

The changeling had once been the Gruagach of Lough Leane, a great shape-shifting wizard and warrior. By the time Hellboy encountered him, the Gruagach had almost none of his former power, and he swore revenge on Hellboy for humiliating him. The Gruagach released the ancient Fomorian giant Grom the War Monster from a long-hidden iron box, and set the huge pig-creature in Hellboy's path. However, Grom ate the Gruagach, trapping the former wizard's spirit in the giant piglike body. Hellboy, aided by Cornelius Agrippa's charm against demonic animals, beat the creature down to the size of a child, and allowed it to escape.

The Gruagach's spirit eventually took control of Grom's body and retreated into the earth to nurse his grudge against Hellboy. His thirst for revenge gradually grew into something more—he saw Hellboy as the chief obstacle to the fairies' reclamation of the earth, which in turn became his sole focus.

In 2002, the Gruagach addressed a council of fairies gathered to discuss the fate of Hellboy, who was being held prisoner at the bottom of the sea by the Bog Roosh. The Gruagach argued that with Hellboy out of the way, the fairies could reclaim dominance over the human world. "Bad enough we have been driven out of the light of day," Gruagach said at that meeting. "Are we so eager to be even less?" Also present was Dagda, the high king of the Irish fairies, one of the most ancient of his race. Dagda believed that the age of the fairies was at an end, and that he would soon gather the last of his race to lead them "down into the shadows under the world."

In April 2005, while Hellboy was still at sea, the Gruagach visited Queen Mab, once the queen of the fairies, now a tiny old woman living under a pile of stones somewhere in England. She told him that Hellboy still lived, and the Gruagach tried to convince her to join him and other fairies who didn't want to follow Dagda into the shadows. Queen Mab warned the Gruagach to be careful of the divisions he was sowing among the fairies. "This thing will echo down the years," she said, "to the ending of us all." The Gruagach responded that he would rather end his time on earth by fighting—"Not to go quiet, not to go unnoticed." He didn't heed Queen Mab's warning, and made his case to the witches of Britain, who, despite their fears, agreed to join his cause against Hellboy.

With the support of the witches, the Gruagach and a handful of allies secured the dismembered remains of an ancient and powerful witch—a Queen of Blood whom they believed would restore the fairies to power. As Dagda cautioned them against restoring the witch queen, he was assassinated by one of the Gruagach's comrades, leaving the Gruagach free to continue with his plans.

HECATE

The queen mother of witches, the goddess of magic, and the keeper of all great dark and secret knowledge, Hecate appeared in some Greek myths as the daughter of the Titans Perses and Asteria, and in others as the daughter of Zeus and Hera. She's a moon goddess and a goddess of the underworld.

Some scholars believe Hecate was in fact an older goddess mentioned in certain ancient texts—Heca-Emem-Ra, the Black Goddess, who was said to have brought about the end of Hyperborea's Golden Age. The Black Goddess was "born out of the shadow of the moon," seduced Thoth (the king during Hyperborea's Golden Age), and "profaned the temple at Gorinium." For that, Thoth cursed her so that she was "half changed in her shape and could no more bear the light of day," a creature half-woman, half-serpent.

The Black Goddess was worshiped in the declining days of Hyperborea, and some believe that she went on to be worshiped under different names in a dozen ancient cultures, including Babylon and Mesopotamia. According to the Roman playwright Gaius Didius, Nero kept a half-woman, half-serpent in a pool of blood in a secret chamber under the Coliseum. Didius claimed that the pool was filled by the blood of the Christians torn to pieces in the games above, and that Emperor Constantine finally drove the creature out of Rome in 313 A.D.

In 1185, Alexis Ampelos, the Greek scholar and author, described Hecate living in a temple on the island of Skyros, attended by devoted priests, and wrote that during the first Inquisition, Christian knights pulled down her temple, but Hecate escaped and hid near the island of Skopelos.

In 1492, Greek fishermen discovered Hecate's petrified body in a sea cave. Mihail Giurescu, a Romanian nobleman traveling in Greece, purchased Hecate's body from the fishermen. He brought her back to his castle and bathed her in ox blood, milk, honey, and oils, until she was restored. Giurescu built Hecate a new temple on his estate and worshiped her. In 1513, Mihail's son Vladimir was thrown from his horse into an icy river and killed; Hecate restored him to life, placing a part of her own soul within him. He became a vampire, and she his Goddess Mother.

For his devoted service to her, Hecate transformed the elderly Mihail into a vampire, granting him eternal life, though not allowing him the youth with which to enjoy it. He declared the area surrounding his castle under her rule. Hecate demanded tribute from him, and for the next five hundred years, Mihail left human sacrifices for her at the cross-roads by the castle, mostly consisting of criminals and travelers passing through the land.

In the early 1800s, Vladimir Giurescu left Romania to fight in the Napoleonic Wars. Several times, he was badly injured in battle. On these occasions, he was brought to Castle Giurescu, where Hecate healed him. In 1944, Vladimir Giurescu left Romania again, this time following Ilsa Haupstein to Germany, where he was killed.

When the body of Giurescu was stolen in 1997, Hellboy was sent to recover it and encountered Hecate at Castle Giurescu. Hecate urged Hellboy to accept his destiny and join her so that together they could "darken the sun, turn the moon to blood, and put out the stars"; in the end the two of them would be alone together, "forever in the dark." Hellboy responded by driving a spear through her chest, and knocking her through a wall, which exposed her to the daylight. The sunlight destroyed her, but a part of her spirit still survived in the newly revived Vladimir Giurescu. As Giurescu faced off in battle against Hellboy, Hecate could see Giurescu was about to be beaten. That remaining part of her spirit abandoned Giurescu's body, destroying him. Nearby, Rasputin had placed Ilsa Haupstein in an iron maiden, a gift from the Baba Yaga. Hecate's spirit entered the iron maiden, taking control of it. In this new form, she confronted Hellboy a second time, again urging him to accept his destiny, and again he refused. He survived the encounter and Hecate disappeared.

In 2001, Hecate appeared to the ghost of Rasputin in the ruins of Hunte Castle in Austria. Rasputin had struggled for years to bring about the destruction of mankind and

the birth of a new human race. She mocked him for his failure, and he became enraged; it's unclear whether she destroyed him or, out of frustration, he destroyed himself.

In 2005, on an island off the coast of Portugal, Hecate appeared to Hellboy a third time, again asking him to join her, to stop the suffering of mankind by ending the world that very instant. When he rejected her this final time, she vanished, promising that they would "be together on the last day, at the ending of the world."

In Italy, in 2006, the magician Igor Bromhead summoned Hecate. Bromhead had acquired the body of Vladimir Giurescu, and forced it to reveal what had become of Hecate at Castle Giurescu: how she had taken over the body of Ilsa Haupstein and the iron maiden. Using Ilsa Haupstein's name to trap Hecate and steal her power, Bromhead entombed her beside the bones of Giurescu.

A short time later, English witches called upon Hecate for guidance in dealing with Hellboy. She did not reply, and they never heard from her again.

HELIOPIC BROTHERHOOD OF RA

and associated groups the Oannes Society and the Osiris Club
See also Langdon Everett Caul

In 1728, Eugene Remy, a previously unremarkable French textile merchant, published a pamphlet claiming that on a recent visit to Egypt, a mysterious being named Larzod had led him to a secret chamber under the Great Pyramid of Cheops. Surrounded by the immense wealth of the ancient king, Larzod revealed to Remy knowledge kept secret since the time of Atlantis, Lemuria, and Mu. Though most of Paris ignored Remy, some were intrigued.

In March 1729, Remy's wealthy patrons financed the purchase of a building in Paris, where Remy established the Temple of Heliopolis. The temple served as the headquarters of the Heliopic Brotherhood of Ra, which Remy founded to preserve the secret teachings of Larzod and pass on the ancient wisdom to those worthy of receiving it.

In 1736, a long-running debate within the H.B.R. reached a boil. While a majority of the Brotherhood believed the Egyptian god Atum—central to Larzod's teachings—to have been self-created, a significant minority held that he was "born from the primal sea." Members who believed in the sea birth split from the Brotherhood and established their own temple a few blocks away. As their symbol, they chose Oannes, a legendary fish-man who supposedly rose from the sea near Babylon to teach primitive men the principles of horticulture and geometry. In 1738, posters all over Paris invited interested parties "seeking to understand the true nature of man" to join the Oannes Society—but a ridiculous drawing of a fish-man on the posters only elicited derision, made worse by a parade and a public ritual on the banks of the Seine conducted by a man in an equally ridiculous Oannes costume. Despite the high hopes of the group, by 1865 their original membership of three hundred had dwindled to less than thirty worldwide. Among those was Langdon Everett Caul, whose undersea explorations in the name of the Society led to his transformation into the fish-man who'd later come to be known as Abe Sapien. Caul's cohorts continued to act in secret, kidnapping the mummy Panya from members of the rival H.B.R. They renamed her Naunet after the Egyptian water goddess, and stole her away to an island in Indonesia, where they lived for over 140 years, as, quite possibly, the last remaining chapter of the Oannes Society. In 1847, the Oannes Society's temple was transformed into an occult bookstore, and was eventually destroyed by fire in 1952.

The Heliopic Brotherhood, by contrast, continued to grow, despite the loss of the Oannes members, the social and political upheaval in France, and the 1745 death of Eugene Remy, who was crushed beneath the wheels of a horse-drawn cart. His body was buried in a specially prepared tomb beneath the streets of Paris. The location of the tomb and the details of the elaborate funeral rituals were among the best-guarded secrets of the Brotherhood.

The H.B.R. supported Napoleon in the years leading up to the French Revolution in 1789, and years later, as a gesture of friendship, Napoleon sent the Brotherhood a gift consisting of artifacts unearthed in a 1798 Egyptian expedition. H.B.R. membership continued to grow, and although it has never been confirmed, Napoleon himself was rumored to have been a secret member.

In 1845, an illiterate thirteen-year-old girl from Nîmes, France, claimed to be the reincarnated Eugene Remy. H.B.R. elders brought the girl to Paris, where she described in detail the location and condition of Remy's tomb and the rituals performed at his burial. The elders accepted her as the second coming of Remy. Renamed Tefnut Trionus, the Queen of Heliopolis, she was the only female ever to be initiated into the Brotherhood.

From 1845 to 1883, Tefnut Trionus held spectacular séances, making wild but often accurate predictions. She also conducted a series of very public affairs with a large number of influential older men, including politicians, artists, and writers, as well as some of the elders of the Brotherhood. She would fall into trances for days at a time, and she often spoke in unknown languages. On several occasions, she walked the streets of Paris naked except for her crown.

During this period, worldwide membership was estimated to be about 40,000, although the actual number may well have been much higher, with a significant number of secret members. This was the Golden Age of the Brotherhood, encompassing both the construction of London's Universal Temple of the H.B.R. in 1857, and the establishment of New York City's Golden Lodge in 1872.

In 1866, Miss E.T. Hatton conducted a séance at the home of Lord Charles Burly in Surrey, England. After the séance, six members of the Brotherhood—including three high-ranking elders—left the H.B.R., forming the Osiris Club with Miss Hatton. The Osiris Club proved to be a genuinely secret society; no one outside the club ever learned what happened during that séance, and to this day it's unknown if the club ever disbanded. There are even rumors that the club still consists of the original seven members from the 1866 séance.

The Golden Age of the H.B.R. ended in 1883, when Queen Tefnut Trionus retired from her position and settled on a small farm in Manitoba, Canada, where she lived quietly with a handful of devoted followers until her death in 1939. Although her position had been purely ceremonial, her retirement led to a series of power struggles within the Brotherhood, and scandals and police investigations caused the H.B.R. to fall from public favor. In 1890, New York's Golden Lodge closed, as did the original H.B.R. temple in Paris. In 1893, the Universal Temple in London closed after an attack by an angry mob.

However, the Brotherhood survived as a highly influential secret society, with Dr. H.W. Carp serving as Grand Master from 1886 to 1897. It's suspected that H.B.R. rituals were responsible for the San Francisco earthquake of 1906, and the Tunguska forest explosion of 1908; however, no further disasters have been connected to the Brotherhood.

The current status of the Heliopic Brotherhood of Ra and the Oannes Society are unknown, but it's feasible that both continue to operate in Europe and the United States.

HELLBOY

On December 23, 1944, a small red demon-like creature appeared in a ball of flames at a ruined church in East Bromwich, England. British and American soldiers, as well as renowned British medium Lady Cynthia Eden-Jones and occult scholars Malcolm Frost and Trevor Bruttenholm, witnessed the event. The creature's appearance coincided exactly with the conclusion of Rasputin's Ragna Rok project, a Nazi-sponsored attempt to release the Ogdru Jahad from their prison in the Abyss.

Sensing that there was more to the creature than its demonic appearance suggested, Trevor Bruttenholm named it Hellboy, and when the Americans took Hellboy to a New Mexico air force base for further study, Bruttenholm accompanied him. With the support of the United States government, Bruttenholm founded the Bureau for Paranormal Research and Defense to investigate occult activities, particularly those related to the Nazis and the Ragna Rok project. At the same time, Bruttenholm continued to work closely with Hellboy, for whom he quickly developed a great deal of affection; in 1946, Bruttenholm officially adopted the two-year-old Hellboy.

In the first two years he had spent in New Mexico, Hellboy had matured at a phenomenal rate. At a week old, he had learned to crawl; within a month, he was walking and talking. Although the American G.I.s on the base initially viewed Hellboy with a mixture of curiosity and fear, they quickly warmed up to him. By his second birthday, they had adopted him as an unofficial mascot, sneaking him into movies and buying him comic books and even a puppy, which he named Mac.

They also (to Bruttenholm's horror and Hellboy's delight) taught him to smoke and play poker.

The military brass were slower to warm up to Hellboy, and even when they grew accustomed to his presence on the base, they viewed him primarily as a research subject and an occasional nuisance. In addition to the Army's scientists, many of the top minds in academics—including such notable figures as J. Robert Oppenheimer, Richard Feynman, and Albert Einstein—were

invited to come study Hellboy (Feynman was eventually banned from the base, after it was discovered that he had taught Hellboy to pick simple locks).

Not everyone shared Bruttenholm's affection for Hellboy. Malcolm Frost, the other occultist who had witnessed Hellboy's appearance, spent most of 1945 traveling and doing research. He returned at the end of that year convinced that Hellboy was a threat to humanity and had to be destroyed. Frost spent the next seven years trying to convince first Bruttenholm—who had already begun the legal process of adopting Hellboy—and then the United States government that Hellboy was too dangerous to be allowed to live. Bruttenholm proceeded with the adoption, and Frost was written off as paranoid.

Throughout, the American government took great pains to keep Hellboy's existence classified, but word of the "kid from hell" eventually leaked out. In 1947, the government grudgingly allowed the press access to Hellboy, who quickly and for a brief period became a media darling. In the wake of the atomic bomb, the public was willing to accept strange phenomena—particularly those connected to the military—and most saw Hellboy as little more than a cute curiosity.

Bruttenholm's duties as head of the new B.P.R.D. often kept him away for weeks at a time. Usually, his work was too dangerous for him to bring Hellboy along, but on several occasions father and son were able to travel together. On one such trip to Africa, in June of 1947, Hellboy wandered away from Bruttenholm and was lost for a full week. Alone on the savannah, he had a vision of a giant rhinoceros who called him Anung Un Rama, something Hellboy kept to himself, and eventually forgot entirely, though he would avoid Africa for many years.

The following month, Hellboy traveled again—this time to the B.P.R.D.'s new headquarters, in Connecticut. There, Bruttenholm began to pay closer attention to Hellboy's formal education, grooming him to be a well-rounded person instead of just a curiosity. He also began bringing Hellboy on actual assignments in the field. Hellboy was extremely bright—he learned almost as quickly as he grew, although he was never particularly eager or adept academically—and by 1952, he was physically and intellectually an adult. That August, after extensive petitioning from Bruttenholm, the United Nations officially recognized Hellboy as an honorary human, which, in turn, allowed him to become an official field agent in the B.P.R.D.

Following Hellboy's promotion, Bruttenholm took him on a two-month father-and-son trip, which gave Bruttenholm a chance to personally instruct Hellboy on investigation techniques and show him more of the world (or at least large parts of the United States and Canada). In 1953, the pair traveled through England, Scotland, and Wales, where Bruttenholm showed Hellboy many of his favorite places and introduced Hellboy to several of Bruttenholm's old friends. The highlight of the trip was when Hellboy and Bruttenholm caught sight of fairies at Calton Hill. Hellboy would later remember his travels with Bruttenholm as the happiest times of his adult life.

However, the opportunity for such trips was increasingly infrequent. As founder and director of the B.P.R.D., Bruttenholm was required to spend most of his time either behind a desk at headquarters, or lobbying for the Bureau's interests in Washington. Hellboy was sent into the field, working alongside other agents on small cases in the U.S. Hellboy proved himself to be a competent field agent, with a superhuman capacity to withstand injury; he could brush off attacks that would have killed an actual human. Hellboy did not, however, display any interest in or skill with research, and his indifference to "book learning" frustrated Bruttenholm.

In 1954, Bruttenholm sent Hellboy to England to meet with members of the mysterious Osiris Club. The Club's motives remained cryptic, but they watched with interest as Hellboy found and fought the St. Leonard's Wyrm. Hellboy was injured during his fight with the dragon, and, unknown to Hellboy, lilies eventually grew up where blood from his wounds touched the ground, echoing the ancient legend of St. Leonard.

In May 1956, Hellboy was sent to Mexico to investigate reports of vampires. There, he teamed up with three wrestler brothers, and the four happily drank and fought monsters together for several months, until one of the brothers was killed. Hellboy disappeared, and, in October, agents were finally sent to retrieve him. They discovered Hellboy passed out drunk in a rundown bar in Morales and brought him home. Hellboy continued to mourn the death of his comrade—the first close friend he had lost in the field—and threw himself back into his work as a distraction.

In March 1959, Hellboy returned to England to investigate a haunted inn. After closing the case, he remained for several months to wander around Britain and Ireland, where he rescued baby Alice Monaghan from the fairies. The Gruagach of Lough Leane, the changeling who had been substituted for baby Alice, would never forgive Hellboy for the injury and insult Hellboy had dealt the Gruagach. This pattern—intensive work followed by travel—became a habit with Hellboy. Every five years or so, he returned to the British Isles to wander, to recuperate from the stress of fieldwork.

Hellboy expressed no interest in investigating his own history and avoided going near the church in East Bromwich where he had first appeared. In May 1962, Cynthia Eden-Jones, one of the occult experts present on the day he had appeared, met with Hellboy and requested that he reopen the investigation of the East Bromwich church. Hellboy refused and continued investigating cases for the B.P.R.D. By 1974, he had traveled through much of the world, although he avoided returning to either Africa or East Bromwich.

One of Hellboy's trips back to B.P.R.D. headquarters coincided with the arrival of Elizabeth Sherman, whose fire-starting powers had recently manifested, killing her immediate family and leveling a city block. At the B.P.R.D., she was cordoned off in a fireproof cell, accessible only to scientists in fireproof HAZMAT suits. Hellboy, who didn't need the protection, was her only real friend and source of physical contact, and his company helped Liz to overcome her trauma, fear, and isolation, and to begin to see the B.P.R.D. as home. The brother-and-sister connection they developed was a source of comfort to them both.

For the next year, Hellboy stayed close to B.P.R.D. headquarters and visited Liz frequently. In late 1975, an outbreak of vampire activity in Budapest took him away from the Fairfield, Connecticut, headquarters, and he remained busy with Bureau

work, although he still checked in on Liz whenever he could. One of his visits in 1979 coincided with the resuscitation of Abe Sapien, the humanoid fish creature, who had arrived at the B.P.R.D. the previous year. As with Liz, Hellboy was the first person in the B.P.R.D. to make "human" contact with Abe, and, when the B.P.R.D. scientists wanted to continue to hold Abe for further study, Hellboy stopped them. Shortly thereafter, Hellboy convinced B.P.R.D. leadership to allow Abe to accompany him on field assignments. Connected by their status as outsiders, the two quickly became close friends.

Unfortunately, their initial partnership was short lived. In June 1979, Hellboy met and fell in love with archaeologist Anastasia Bransfield and decided to all but abandon B.P.R.D. work to travel with her. Their romance strained Hellboy's relationship with

Trevor Bruttenholm, who disapproved but respected Hellboy's autonomy. The romance lasted until 1981 when Hellboy, concerned that the relationship was costing Anastasia the respect of her peers, broke it off.

Searching for a distraction, Hellboy threw himself into his work, but his mind remained elsewhere. In late August 1982, after he had destroyed several city blocks in an explosion while fighting a vampire in Prague, it became clear that Hellboy needed a break from fieldwork, and he once again retreated to England for several months before returning to his regular work with the Bureau.

In late 1992, Hellboy was surprised to learn that Trevor Bruttenholm had joined the Cavendish Arctic Expedition. Though their relationship had been tested by Hellboy's involvement with Bransfield, Hellboy and Bruttenholm had always been extremely close, and Hellboy was hit hard by the expedition's disappearance in January 1993. True to character, he tried to distract himself from worry by throwing himself into his work.

On August 16, 1993, on a visit to the New York City Explorers' Club, Hellboy experienced a mystical vision. While looking at a mummy retrieved from a mysterious African ruin, Hellboy first remembered his earlier experience in Africa, then "saw" himself as an African folk hero named Makoma, experiencing the hero's life and his death. The mummy itself crumbled to dust. Hellboy, blamed for the destruction of the mummy, was subsequently banned from the Explorers' Club.

The following May, Hellboy received further insight into his origins and purpose. Trevor Bruttenholm reappeared and asked Hellboy to meet him at Bruttenholm's Brooklyn apartment. Hellboy came immediately, but had only just arrived when a frog creature appeared and killed Bruttenholm. Bruttenholm's death and the subsequent investigation set in motion a series of events that changed the course of Hellboy's life.

Working with Liz and Abe, Hellboy tracked the frog creatures to Cavendish Hall in upstate New York, where he discovered that Rasputin was planning to bring about the destruction of mankind, the birth of a "new race," and the freeing of the Ogdru Jahad. Rasputin claimed to be Hellboy's "true father," announcing that it was he who had summoned Hellboy to earth to command the powers that Rasputin wanted to unleash on the world.

Even after Hellboy, Abe, and Liz had defeated Rasputin, the sorceror still claimed to be Hellboy's master, and told him that if he destroyed Rasputin, he would never find out who he truly was or the true nature of his power. Hellboy responded by destroying Rasputin's corporeal body and crushing his skull to dust. As Hellboy later told Abe, "I'm red, I've got horns, hooves, and a tail. It's not like he was going to tell me anything good."

However, his encounter with Rasputin had left Hellboy with a lingering curiosity about his origin and nature. Following Bruttenholm's funeral in England, he decided to return to the East Bromwich church for the first time. While sleeping in the ruins of the church, Hellboy woke to a vision of a witch who repented her sins on her

deathbed. He saw her two children, a monk and a nun, place her dead body in a coffin, which they chained shut and placed inside the church in accordance with her last request. Then, a demon with whom the witch had once consorted came to the church. It incinerated the monk and nun and claimed the witch as his own, telling her that she was carrying his child—a son, his favorite son. With those words, the demon turned and stared directly at Hellboy, then chained the witch to his horse, and rode off, presumably to hell. Hellboy tried to write off what he had seen as no more than a dream, but he knew that he had witnessed a real event, and that he was the child that the demon—his father—had spoken of. Aside from a letter to Abe, he told no one of the vision and threw himself back into his work.

In 1997, the remains of the vampire Vladimir Giurescu were stolen from a New York City wax museum, and Hellboy was sent to Romania to recover them before they could be restored to life. At Castle Giurescu, Hellboy battled the goddess Hecate, who, much like Rasputin, told Hellboy that it was his destiny to join her, to "darken the sun, turn the moon to blood, and put out the stars" and "ring down the curtain on man." Hellboy rejected her offer as well, and ultimately destroyed her, as he had Rasputin.

Shortly thereafter, Hecate returned, this time in the form of an iron maiden containing the body of Ilsa Haupstein. She showed Hellboy the Ogdru Jahad in their prison in the Abyss, and the darkness itself spoke to Hellboy, calling him by his true name—Anung Un Rama, World Destroyer. It told him that he was born to loose the Dragon; that he must wake his "devil heart" and don his "crown of fire" and that his "coming of age [would be] the death knell of man." Determined to be master of his own destiny, Hellboy rejected the darkness's demand that he choose between death and life as the destroyer of the world, breaking off his newly grown horns and returning to earth unharmed. Sir Edward, a masked figure who watched the confrontation from a distance with the Baba Yaga and the elf king Dagda, commented that Hellboy, "born of human woman in hell and reborn of human design on earth . . . now, finally [had given] birth to himself."

After the fight at Castle Giurescu, Hellboy remained in Romania with B.P.R.D. agent Kate Corrigan to track down a homunculus that had stolen Liz's fire, without which she was dying. They found and captured the homunculus at Czege Castle, and Hellboy convinced the creature—which he had named Roger—to return Liz's fire, saving her life. Although the exchange returned Roger to a lifeless state, the homunculus was later revived and eventually became an agent of the B.P.R.D.

In 1998, a dying priest, the son of the same Malcolm Frost who had witnessed Hellboy's appearance, contacted Hellboy and requested a meeting. Frost's son gave Hellboy an ancient parchment once owned by Frost, which showed a stylized image of Hellboy's enormous right hand. Below the image, in ancient Lemurian text, was inscribed the phrase, "Behold the Right Hand of Doom." This, the priest told Hellboy, had been the catalyst for Frost's campaign to have Hellboy destroyed. Hellboy, in turn, told the priest about his own experiences at Cavendish Hall and East Bromwich, and about Hecate and the voice that had told him to "wake the Dragon." He hoped that the priest might offer him some reassurance or reprieve from his destiny; instead, the priest told Hellboy that the right hand was his burden

to carry, and that even though Hellboy himself might not be tempted to use it, it was his duty to keep it safe from those who would.

Hellboy returned to his work, and for a time, he was able to put the priest's words out of his mind. However, in 1999, while investigating the theft of an iron box and tongs stolen by the smuggler Igor Bromhead, Hellboy encountered Ualac, a minor demon with lofty ambitions. Bromhead and Ualac trapped Hellboy and used magic to manifest the previously invisible crown of the apocalypse that hovered above Hellboy's head.

When Ualac placed the crown on his own head, it transformed him into the thing that Hellboy was supposed to have been—Anung Un Rama, the Destroyer. Ualac intended to also take Hellboy's right hand, calling it a "great and ancient thing," and claiming that it would not only be able to "loose the Dragon," but also to "breathe life into the lifeless soldiers of hell and set that army to war against heaven."

Hellboy defeated Ualac and turned the minor demon over to Astaroth, a Grand Duke of Hell whom Bromhead had summoned. Astaroth returned Ualac to prison and offered to return Hellboy's crown. Hellboy refused, and Astaroth replied that it would be kept for him "in Hell, in Pandemonium, in the House of the Fly." Before he left, Astaroth told Hellboy that a seat in hell was already waiting for him.

A few days after this incident, Hellboy confided in Kate Corrigan, one of his closest friends in the B.P.R.D. He asked her what would happen to him if he were to face the mystery of his life and set out to investigate his true origins. Hellboy expected Kate to reassure him and convince him to remain at the B.P.R.D.; instead, she encouraged him to explore his purpose and destiny on earth. Ignoring her advice and casting aside the parchment that the priest had given him, Hellboy tried one last time to return to work.

Hellboy's final investigation as an agent of the B.P.R.D. took place in 2001, in Austria. Hellboy and Roger were sent to the ruins of Hunte Castle to investigate the possible return of a Nazi space capsule launched from the site in 1939. There, Hellboy encountered an alien who had apparently been living on the earth for almost fifty years, disguised as a human being. The alien had been present at the church in East Bromwich on the night that Hellboy was "born." It had been sent to prevent Hellboy from growing up and destroying the earth. But the alien had recognized in the infant Hellboy the potential for free will, and he believed that Hellboy would be able to choose his own path in life; seeing this, he decided to risk letting Hellboy live.

This encounter, coupled with Hellboy's discovery prior to the mission that the B.P.R.D. had implanted a bomb inside Roger, convinced Hellboy that it was time to leave the Bureau. When the Hunte Castle mission concluded, he walked away from the B.P.R.D., planning to travel "wherever the wind blows." The alien had told him that to be other than human is not to be less; Hellboy was ready to discover that for himself.

Faintly recalling his 1993 vision in the Explorers' Club, Hellboy decided to return to Africa for the first time since his childhood. For more than a year, he wandered aimlessly around the continent. Eventually, he decided to seek out the great witch doctor Mohlomi, whom he finally discovered squatting in the middle of an otherwise-empty savannah. Mohlomi gave Hellboy a powerful amulet—a magical bell—and then magically transported him to the coast of Africa, where Hellboy was abducted by mermaids, taken to the bottom of the ocean, and turned over to the Bog Roosh, an ancient sea witch. The Bog Roosh intended to kill Hellboy, destroying the threat his right hand posed to the world, but Hellboy escaped. For a few years, he drifted in the ocean, finally washing up on a tiny island surrounded by wrecked ships, somewhere off the coast of Portugal, in 2005.

On the island, Hellboy spent some time drinking with the ghosts of the dead sailors, until Hecate found him there. She called to him, asking him again to accept his destiny. She told him that a great disaster was coming, and that everyone he had loved and cared for would die slow and tortuous deaths. The end was inevitable, she claimed, asking Hellboy to join with her and avoid the suffering. A word from him could end everything in an instant. He rejected her, and she disappeared, saying that they would be together, "on the last day, at the ending of the world."

Later that night, Hellboy encountered the creature Urgo-Hem, one of the Ogdru Hem, and was impaled on the creature's leg, and apparently bled to death from the wound. A Spanish priest who had been killed on the island in 1525 re-created himself from Hellboy's blood. Aided by the magic bell given to him by Mohlomi,

Hellboy was able to return to life, and the newly revived priest told him a brief version of the Secret History of the World—including the tale of the watcher angel Anum, who had both created the Ogdru Jahad and imprisoned them in the Abyss. Anum had been destroyed by his fellow angels, but his right hand had survived. The hand had become a sacred object in Hyperborea, where it was incorporated into a statue. One day, the statue came to life to kill corrupt priests, and then destroyed itself, but its right hand remained. This was Hellboy's hand—the Right Hand of Doom.

The priest had wanted to prepare mankind to survive the return of the Ogdru Hem, but because his body was formed from Hellboy's blood, he turned into a demon. Hellboy was able to destroy the priest-demon and Urgo-Hem at the same time.

After Hellboy left the island, storms drove him south, and he remained lost at sea for another two years before finally washing up on the west coast of England. There,

he made his way to his old friend Harry Middleton's house, where he remained for three months.

In the meantime, Igor Bromhead had summoned and imprisoned Hecate, leaving the witches of the world without a leader. Because of Hellboy's heritage—his mother had been a witch, and his father had been lord over witches—the witches summoned Hellboy to their gathering. They asked him to become their king, cautioning him not to turn them down "lest there be war between us." Hellboy refused, but when he left the church, instead of returning to England, he appeared in a snowstorm, where he found the Baba Yaga waiting for him. She told him that he had strayed to the "wider world," and that she would now have revenge for the loss of her eye—to which end she had raised an enormous skeletal army.

Hellboy survived the army's first assault with the help of Perun, "King of the World," an old Russian god. Then he was attacked by Koshchei the Deathless, an ancient warrior whom the Baba Yaga had promised his soul—and the release of death—if Koshchei killed Hellboy and delivered his eye to the Baba Yaga. Hellboy evaded Koshchei with the help of another ally—the girl Vasilisa—whom Koshchei then killed. Finally, Koshchei was able to strike a killing blow against Hellboy—

but Hellboy proved "as deathless as Koshchei." Finally, armed with a magical comb and hand-kerchief from Vasilisa, Hellboy was able to defeat Koshchei and escape. Back in England, he was confronted by seventeenth-century witch hunter Henry Hood; however, Hood's body dissolved to ash, leaving Hood's sword—inscribed with the name "Bromhead"—behind.

With the sword, Hellboy tracked down Igor Bromhead. Bromhead begged Hellboy to kill him and end his misery, and Hellboy complied. As he died, Bromhead described a vision of hell—with Hellboy astride a dragon, at the head of a great army.

HERMAN VON KLEMPT

Brilliant scientist and surgeon Herman von Klempt was born in 1885, in Frankfurt, Germany. His interest in cybernetics—the combination of organic and machine parts to create new, efficient beings—was first displayed when, at ten years old, he killed the family cat and tried to improve its design by integrating clock parts into its body. His ghoulish experiments and apparent lack of concern for life frightened his family, and when he announced his intention to attend medical school in Berlin, they were relieved to be rid of him.

In Berlin, von Klempt's single-minded dedication to his experiments rapidly earned him a reputation as obsessive, and something of a loose cannon. At medical school, von Klempt attached himself to an older student, Karl Kroenen. While Kroenen was genuinely fond of von Klempt, von Klempt saw Kroenen as little more than a resource to be exploited; Kroenen's wealth and social connections provided economic backing for research von Klempt could never otherwise have performed. He and Kroenen performed a wide range of experiments during their years at medical school; most of these involved the creation of animal-machine hybrids.

Around 1920, Kroenen was severely injured in a laboratory explosion. Seeing his future funding slip away along with Kroenen's life—and sensing a valuable opportunity to test some of his more radical theories on a human—von Klempt used his experimental transplantation techniques to save Kroenen's life. The details and extent of the procedures von Klempt performed are unknown, but Kroenen was never again seen in public without his body and face fully covered.

In 1935, von Klempt and Kroenen were invited to join Himmler's new Sonnenrad Society, also known as the German Occult Bureau, based in Berlin. Von Klempt had made the most of Kroenen's resources, developing his own private kriegaffe (war-ape) project, but he now hoped that Sonnenrad would fund his and Kroenen's dream project—a super army of half-man, half-machine soldiers. In the spring of 1936, the Sonnenrad Society established a lab for the development of the army in Hunte Castle in Austria.

Shortly after he joined the Occult Bureau, von Klempt used his new status to court and marry a local girl—less out of affection than his desire to establish a social image as more than just "Kroenen's ugly friend." However, the marriage was short-lived. In 1936, von Klempt was nearly killed in a laboratory explosion. Kroenen, working with other members of the Occult Bureau, managed to keep von Klempt's severed head alive in a bell jar; how much of this achievement was science and how much magic remains unknown. Shortly after, von Klempt's wife went to live with family in Vienna, and the two never spoke again.

Von Klempt quickly adjusted to life as a disembodied head. He channeled his love of robotics into the development of a wide range of mechanical prosthetics. Despite his relative handicap of being a head in a jar, this was one of the most fruitful periods of von Klempt's life.

In 1937, Rasputin invited Kroenen to join him on the Ragna Rok project—one of many Nazi doomsday projects—while von Klempt remained at Hunte Castle. On March 20, 1939, U.S. troops, accompanied by The Lobster, infiltrated Hunte Castle, which also housed the Nazi space program. The battle resulted in an explosion that sent fire sweeping through the castle. Von Klempt, protected by his jar, was the sole survivor, although his mechanical body was badly damaged, and his prized experiments destroyed. He returned to Germany, where he was outfitted with a new body and continued to work on his research until the end of the war.

With the fall of the Third Reich imminent, von Klempt began planning for his own future and accumulating the means to continue his work. He secreted generators and other equipment in a hidden bunker, and, in the chaos following the fall of Berlin, he and his Kriegaffen #1 and #2 moved one hundred of the subjects of Project Vampir Sturm—a failed doomsday project meant to create an army of vampires—to his new laboratory. There, he attempted to revive the failed rocket program in order to launch the vampires into the heart of the United States. The plan was foiled by Trevor Bruttenholm and a small company of American and Soviet troops, and von Klempt was forced to abandon his body to avoid capture. He arranged for his head to be smuggled to a jungle in South America, where he was able to find enough funding from Nazi sympathizers and survivors of the Third Reich to continue his experiments.

In August 1959, von Klempt was living in Brazil, near Macapa, in the ruins of an abandoned villa. His Kriegaffe prototype #9—which von Klempt had named Brutus—had been kidnapping local girls and using their spinal fluid to replenish the solution that kept von Klempt's head alive and healthy. The desiccated bodies of the girls had begun to wash up on the banks of the Amazon; because the bodies had puncture wounds in their necks, the locals suspected that a vampire was

responsible. The B.P.R.D. sent Hellboy to investigate. Hellboy destroyed Brutus and left von Klempt for dead.

Although Hellboy had severely damaged von Klempt's jar, the scientist survived in a state of semi-suspended animation for the next thirty-eight years. In 1997, Roderick Zinco, the C.E.O. of Zinco Laboratories, retrieved von Klempt's head on the orders of Kroenen, who had himself woken from hibernation only a few years before. In Norway, Kroenen revived von Klempt, hoping that the two of them could work together again—this time, toward Rasputin's goal of Ragna Rok. Scornful of Kroenen's allegiance to the dead Rasputin, von Klempt tried to convince him to return to South America, where von Klempt's old projects— any one of which, he claimed, could make them the most powerful men in the world—still waited. "Why burn down the world," he asked Kroenen, "when we can be its masters?"

Before von Klempt could convince Kroenen to abandon Rasputin, Leopold Kurtz, another of Rasputin's inner circle, overheard von Klempt's seditious words and attacked him with a wrench. In the ensuing chaos, Kroenen stabbed Kurtz, and shortly thereafter, the castle was destroyed in an explosion. All within were presumed dead.

Once again, von Klempt managed to survive. He fled to South America, only to find all of his colleagues long dead and his secret projects in ruin. Completely alone for the first time, von Klempt made his way back to Germany and returned to a secret workshop under the cemetery near Ingolstadt that he and Kroenen had once shared. There, he gathered the materials to build a new Kriegaffe, but as the ape neared completion, von Klempt was overwhelmed by crippling despair. In his despair, von Klempt heard a voice that he believed belonged to the Angel of Death (actually Rasputin's ghost). Rasputin told von Klempt that he had been chosen to do great things and divulged to him the secret behind the Nazi space program: the dead body of Nazi physicist Ernst Oeming had been launched into space in 1939, intended as a vessel for the Conqueror Worm, one of the disembodied Ogdru Hem. Rasputin also told von Klempt that after she had left him, his wife had given birth to von Klempt's son, and von Klempt now had a granddaughter, Inger, who was loyal to the Nazi cause. Inger had infiltrated the Austrian secret police under the name Laura Karnstein, and she was happy to have the chance to assist her legendary grandfather with his new work.

At von Klempt's bidding, she assembled neo-Nazi troops and equipment at Hunte Castle, while von Klempt made radio contact with the Nazi spacecraft containing Oeming's remains and recalled it to earth. He had never believed in Rasputin's epic vision, but he was bitter from defeat and disappointment and eager to play a role in the destruction of the world that had wronged him.

The capsule landed and the Conqueror Worm—actually one of the Ogdru Hem— was released. However, the B.P.R.D. had sent Hellboy and Roger the Homunculus to investigate the capsule's return. Roger defeated the Ogdru Hem, then jumped off the wall of Hunte Castle, holding von Klempt's head. The jar shattered to pieces on the rocks, and von Klempt is assumed to have been killed on impact, though his head has never been found.

IGOR BROMHEAD

Igor Weldon Bromhead was born in 1947, in an upper-class Philadelphia suburb. His father, Maxwell Kingsley Bromhead, was a cousin to English nobility who had fled England during World War II to set up a law practice in Philadelphia. There, he had married Olga Yudenich, the granddaughter of a Russian count who had escaped the Russian Revolution in 1917 as part of the White Émigré.

When Bromhead was seventeen years old, he ran away from his life of privilege to experience the free love and psychedelic drugs of 1960s San Francisco. However, instead of becoming part of the scene, Bromhead quickly recognized the business potential of the hippie movement. Establishing himself as a drug dealer rather than a user, he developed a reputation in the Bay Area as the person to go to for exotic drugs. He sought clients with backgrounds similar to his own, selling diluted product and making a profit off what he called "the weak, over-privileged children of upper-middle-class America."

Bromhead's own upper-class background and his ability to deliver exotic substances gained him the attention of the more bizarre parts of San Francisco counterculture, including the occult community. Ever the entrepreneur, Bromhead recognized that talismans and spells could be as profitable as drugs. There was no end to the money his clients would spend in their search for "genuine" occult experiences, and Bromhead learned that merely teasing them with the possibility of such experiences would yield heavy profits and return customers. He began to study the occult and quickly learned to fake skills he did not actually possess—mostly communing with the dead and telling fortunes. When his dealings led him into a graveyard ritual performed by "Professor" William Whitcomb, a true practitioner of the black arts, Bromhead discovered that there was real, dangerous magic in the world, and for years he was careful to avoid it.

Instead, Bromhead continued to con the wealthy and the curious, charging large fees to lift invented curses and read fortunes, and selling expensive charms and potions. In 1971, he opened a shop in Haight-Ashbury, offering "magical services and artifacts." While he promoted his merchandise as exotic herbs and potions "from all around the world," he usually assembled them himself, from ingredients that were both local and cheap.

By 1975, however, Bromhead had become a world traveler, and his ambitions and increasing expertise in the field took him from overpriced forgeries to truly valuable items. He became a middleman in a worldwide ring of smugglers, trafficking merchandise stolen from tombs and temples in Africa and Asia and from private collections in Europe. Many of these objects possessed real, otherworldly power. Bromhead continued his studies in the occult, learning various ways to protect himself from the dangerous merchandise that had become his stock in trade.

Though Bromhead's genius as a con man kept him out of the way of traditional law enforcement, his business attracted the attention of the B.P.R.D., which kept tabs on the occult smugglers' ring in which he was involved. Hellboy ran into Bromhead more than once, but since Bromhead was "one of a thousand fake fortune tellers and con men" whose interests were in separating willing customers from their money, the Bureau had no cause to interfere with him.

In February 1983, Bromhead arranged for the theft of a powerful magical object: the left ring finger of prominent Elizabethan magician John Dee. Bromhead had stolen the finger from the reliquary at a church that Hellboy was investigating in connection with a number of missing college students. Hellboy caught Bromhead red-handed, exposing a series of thefts and fraud that led to a fifteen-year jail sentence for the con man. For Hellboy, Bromhead's indictment was simply another day's work, and he didn't give the smuggler a second thought.

Despite his life of crime, Bromhead had a lot in common with "the weak, over-privileged children of upper-middle-class America" on whom he'd preyed, and prison was hard on him. His experiences behind bars caused him to turn to the black arts for protection, and he earnestly studied magic until his release in 1998.

Bromhead still had his smuggling connections, but he was leery of anything that might send him back to prison. During his years in jail, he'd dreamed of one final score that would finance his retirement. His connections in the black market led him to the perfect dupes: Count and Countess Guarino in Lockmaben, Scotland, who were spending a fortune on occult artifacts. Bromhead traveled to Scotland, intent on squeezing as much money from them as possible.

The Guarinos had already squandered the majority of their fortune, but Bromhead still saw them as his ticket to wealth. The Count and Countess were devout Satanists, determined to see the devil in their lifetimes, and they were willing to give their last shilling to Bromhead to make it happen. He strung them along for months with fake spirit communication, but with their wealth running out and their single-minded interest in "bringing the devil forth out of his fiery hell," Bromhead knew he'd have to deliver better than spurious ghosts.

He recalled a story he'd heard during his smuggling days about a minor demon whom St. Dunstan had imprisoned in an iron box and sealed in a wall in an English manor. There'd been a time when Bromhead wouldn't have considered getting so close to an actual demon, but he found himself compelled to take this chance. Through his old black-market connections and a little direct thievery, Bromhead obtained the box and, as a measure of security, learned the demon's true name—Ualac.

According to a version of the legend—which Bromhead passed on to the Guarinos as fact—St. Dunstan had imprisoned not a minor demon, but the devil himself. The Guarinos were overjoyed and happily exchanged their remaining wealth, including their home, for the box that they believed to contain the devil. They thought that they'd be rewarded (either on earth or in hell) for setting Satan free; instead, as soon as the box was opened, the Countess was possessed and physically transformed into Ualac. Ualac cursed Count Guarino, turning him into a monkey, and tried to turn Bromhead into a lizard. However, Bromhead was protected by a charm depicting St. Dunstan.

Armed with the demon's secret name, and using the iron tongs Dunstan had originally used to trap the demon, Bromhead demanded that Ualac grant him great wealth and power. The demon replied that there was a treasure hidden in the basement of the house Bromhead now owned, and that, if he wanted true power, he would help the demon trap the Great Beast—Hellboy.

Over the centuries that Ualac had been trapped in the box, he'd been able to hear whispers from hell and from the Abyss where the Ogdru Jahad were held prisoner. He'd learned that Hellboy was "The Great Beast, Harbinger of the Apocalypse." Ualac wanted to take Hellboy's crown for himself. From the box, Ualac had devised and executed a plan to lure Hellboy to him: as Bromhead left the house where Ualac's box had been hidden, Ualac implanted an image of the Guarinos' mansion in the mind of the house's owner. He, in turn, passed on the location to Hellboy and Abe Sapien, who were investigating the theft of the box.

Abe and Hellboy arrived at the Guarino home shortly after Ualac was set free. Bromhead used Hellboy's secret name—provided by Ualac—to gain power over Hellboy and, with a spell Ualac had taught him, he made Hellboy's hidden crown of the apocalypse appear. Ualac took the crown and became the Beast of the Apocalypse himself.

Bromhead, unconcerned with crowns, tried to take revenge on Hellboy for putting him in prison, but Ualac stopped him before he could kill Hellboy. When Hellboy eventually freed himself, Bromhead fled, calling on Astaroth, one of the major lords of hell, for assistance. In the confusion that followed, the bottom half of Bromhead's Saint Dunstan charm broke off. Without the charm's full protection, the curse that Ualac had tried to put on Bromhead took partial effect, leaving the con man with lizard legs and a tail.

With Hellboy and Abe focused on Ualac and Astaroth, Bromhead was able to get away, hiding in the secret treasure-laden passageways under the Guarino mansion. Now that he had touched real, powerful magic, Bromhead could never go back to his previous way of life. Having secured enough of Guarino's money to finance the retirement he'd previously dreamed of, he now focused on gaining the power to lash out at a world that he blamed for his misfortunes.

Through his contacts in occult circles and in the black market, Bromhead learned about the skeleton of Vladimir Giurescu, which had been stolen from a Romanian airport several years before. In 1999, Bromhead spent a sizable chunk of the Guarino fortune to acquire the skeleton, and to have it brought to the catacombs near Lucca, Italy, where the half-lizard con man was living in secret with the help of a small group of local servants whom he paid to bring him food and other necessities.

With little experience practicing necromancy, it took Bromhead years to contact Giurescu's spirit, and to recall that spirit into the bones. Giurescu's spirit was angry at Ilsa Haupstein for jilting him in favor of the ghost of Rasputin, an act which had left Giurescu himself to be destroyed by Hellboy. The spirit told Bromhead everything that had happened at Castle Giurescu in 1997, about Ilsa, Hecate, and the iron maiden.

In March 2007, Bromhead killed his servants in a blood offering to summon Hecate. Knowing that she was now, at her core, Ilsa Haupstein, Bromhead used that secret name to trap her. He believed he could take Hecate's power for himself and become the lord over all the witches of the world.

However, Hecate's power proved too much for Bromhead to contain or control. His body warped even further, and the would-be necromancer remained hidden near Lucca until Hellboy finally tracked him down. Bromhead begged Hellboy to kill him and end his misery, and Hellboy complied. As he died, Bromhead described a vision of hell—with Hellboy astride a dragon, at the head of a great army.

ILSA HAUPSTEIN

On June 7, 1919, Ilsa Haupstein was born in a nondescript house in the country-side two hours east of Berlin, the third and last daughter of a mid-level country bureaucrat and a good German housewife. Ilsa's first years were remarkable only in that even as an infant, Ilsa never cried.

Ilsa's early childhood passed without incident. When she was ten, her teacher noticed that Ilsa possessed an uncanny natural athletic ability and recommended the child to an elite gymnastics program in Berlin. Ilsa was soon sent to study under Germany's top coaches, in the country's most advanced training facility. As Ilsa grew, so did her gymnastic ability. By thirteen, Ilsa had won every major competition in her league, and it was often said that she was the best gymnast her country had ever produced.

But Ilsa's success was short lived: in 1933, as Ilsa was completing a complicated dismount from the uneven parallel bars, the upper bar broke. Ilsa fell, fracturing four ribs and a hip, and puncturing her lung. A later investigation proved that the bar had been sabotaged by an unscrupulous competitor. Less than a year later, the saboteur was found dead in her dormitory bathroom. Ilsa was questioned concerning her death, but no formal charges were ever filed.

Although her injuries would prevent her from competing again, Ilsa remained active in the gymnastics league, serving as an administrator in the Berlin offices until she was seventeen. On her seventeenth birthday, Ilsa transferred from the gymnastics league offices to the Nazi party headquarters, where she worked as the secretary to the undersecretary to Nazi brass Heinrich Himmler.

In December 1936, six months into her post, Ilsa's immediate superior was found dead in his bathroom. Ilsa was promoted to take his place and soon caught the eye of Himmler himself. After putting her through a series of grueling tests, Himmler brought her into the inner circle of his new German Occult Bureau.

Under Himmler, Ilsa came into contact with the most brilliant minds in the Nazi party, including Professor Doctors Herman von Klempt, Ernst Oeming, Gunter Eiss, Karl Ruprect Kroenen, and Leopold Kurtz. She was instrumental in the planning of both Oeming's atomic-bomb experiments and his eventual assassination, as well as the attempt to launch his body into space. Her ideas also proved key to the continuing recruitment of Nazi scientists and the discovery of such notable occult artifacts as the robe of Christ and the Spear of Longinus.

The turning point of Ilsa's years with Himmler was meeting Grigori Yefimovich Rasputin. Himmler had recruited Rasputin in 1937, but kept his name secret from the members of his Occult Bureau throughout the war. Though the mysterious Russian kept mainly to himself, he gradually took Ilsa into his confidence, telling her that his purpose was far beyond that which he had promised Himmler. He told her that he would set in motion events to change the world completely, bringing about "a new world and a New Race of Men." Ilsa was fascinated, although she still didn't realize the full extent of her mysterious master's plans, or their cosmic origins with the Ogdru Jahad. Rasputin called his plan Ragna Rok and selected Ilsa, along with Occult Bureau members Leopold Kurtz and Professor Doctor Karl Ruprect Kroenen, to spearhead the project.

Ilsa worked on Ragna Rok from 1938 through 1944, when she left with the blessings of both Himmler and Rasputin to head up a delegation to Castle Giurescu in Romania, to enlist the vampire Giurescu in Germany's war effort. The new project, called Vampir Sturm, was to facilitate the creation of a vampire army. To create such an army, Himmler needed a vampire like Vladimir Giurescu, one powerful enough to create others. Before Ilsa's delegation could reach the castle, they were attacked by crows on the outskirts of Giurescu's land. Ilsa was the sole survivor of the attack.

She spent thirty days at Castle Giurescu, focusing all of her substantial powers on convincing Giurescu to return with her to Berlin. Ilsa had had romantic affairs before—affairs in which she was always entirely in control—but she'd never met a man like Giurescu. Her true master, Rasputin, was a godlike personality, to whom she could never relate—whose name she still didn't even know; Giurescu, on the other hand, was stronger than any man she'd ever met, but still a man in many ways. He seduced Ilsa, much to the displeasure of his six wives.

In October of 1944, Giurescu brought his wives with him to Germany, to meet with Himmler. Considering her mission complete, Ilsa left Germany the next morning to help with preparations for the Ragna Rok project on Tarmagant Island. Ilsa and Giurescu had planned to meet back in Berlin when the war was won, but it was not to be. On December 3, Giurescu was summoned for a private conference with Hitler at Wewelsburg Castle. Shortly thereafter, and unbeknownst to Ilsa, Hitler issued orders for the arrest and execution of Giurescu and his wives.

On December 23, 1944, at the moment that the Ragna Rok project seemed to fail, Ilsa had a vision of a flame dancing above her master's head, spelling out his true name: Rasputin. Shortly thereafter, Rasputin revealed that Giurescu had been killed six days earlier at Dachau.

Rasputin promised Ilsa, Kurtz, and Kroenen that their faith would save them, and ordered them to go into hiding. With Giurescu dead, Ragna Rok an apparent failure, and the German state in shambles, Ilsa traveled with her two compatriots to Kroenen's ancestral home in Norway, where they placed themselves in cryogenic stasis. They remained frozen until the moment of Rasputin's death in May 1994.

For two months, Ilsa and her comrades awaited a sign from Rasputin. Finally, a message came in the form of Roderick Zinco, an American businessman who had pledged his vast wealth to revive Rasputin's Ragna Rok project.

With Zinco's money, Kroenen and Kurtz began creating an army. Ilsa traveled alone to New York, on a personal mission to recover the corpse of Vladimir Giurescu, which she had tracked to a wax museum owned by former Nazi officer Hans Ubler. Ilsa shot and killed Ubler and reclaimed Giurescu's body, which she brought to the castle in Romania where they had first met, and where, under the light of the full moon, his corpse could be revived.

With Kurtz and Kroenen busy in Norway, Ilsa was free to revive the vampire and make the world suffer for his death. But before Giurescu was revived, Rasputin's ghost appeared to Ilsa. He told Ilsa that as a spirit he had been free to travel into the Dark behind the Stars, to the "Pit," and to commune with the imprisoned Ogdru

Jahad. He told her of his early life as a man and how he had been "reborn in chaos." Finally, he offered her the chance to be reborn, to become the Destroyer of Mankind. Ilsa agreed.

As Ilsa pledged her faith to her master, an iron maiden sent by the Baba Yaga rose from the ground. Rasputin told Ilsa that this would be her new body, for the "times that are coming will be too harsh for flesh." She would need to stand beside him "in the teeth of the Ragna Rok storm," and she would have to "die a little" to receive the great power of the Dragon.

Ilsa stepped willingly inside. As the door to the iron maiden closed on her, and Ilsa was pierced through with spikes, the face of the iron maiden wept tears of blood. A short time later, the iron maiden, with Ilsa's body still inside, was possessed by the spirit of Hecate. The iron maiden became Hecate's physical form, but what became of Ilsa Haupstein after the iron maiden closed on her—whether her spirit was destroyed, or remains there as part of Hecate—is unknown.

JOHANN KRAUS

J ohann Kraus was born in Stuttgart, Germany, in
1946. He began to be aware of his psychic
abilities when he was ten years old, when he started
to see people that others could not and slowly
realized that these were ghosts. He often saw a
wounded German soldier standing in the garden
of his family home, clearly suffering and very
sad. Johann was frustrated that he could not
communicate with the soldier, to find out what
was wrong, and possibly to help.

This frustration eventually led him to investigate
spiritualism. Studying under an elderly German
woman, Anneliese Steiner, he participated in a
number of séances, and witnessed a series of bizarre
manifestations, most notably thirty-two Roman
soldiers who appeared in Steiner's house one
evening; some of the soldiers milled around for
several days afterward. Johann met other spiritualists
through Steiner and was exposed to a variety of
occult studies. Ultimately, he didn't like the direction
of the group and cut himself off from his mentor.

His frustration with occultism led Johann back
to the church, which allowed him to focus again
on the spirits themselves, whom he continued
to see and wanted to help. On his own, he learned how to communicate with
them, and eventually to send his own spirit out of his body and onto the etheric
plane, where he could commune with the departed. He also learned how to let
those spirits speak through him, and to get them to assume temporary physical
forms made of ectoplasm, a substance mostly composed of fluid from the medium's body.

In 1971, Johann opened a small office in Munich, where he became a well-respected
medium before relocating to Heidelberg. His one professional lapse came when he
fell in love with the spirit of a dead woman when he was supposed to be trying to
help her living husband come to terms with his grief. Throughout, his genuine
interest in helping the departed and their loved ones set him apart from many
other mediums who exploited tragedies. While he made his living as a medium,
he was known to help people regardless of their financial situations.

In February 2002, in Chengdou Province, China, a thief broke into a warehouse holding occult objects seized by a secret branch of the Chinese government. The thief tried to open a small jade figurine, unwittingly releasing a massive burst of psychic energy that killed everyone within a hundred miles and sent a shock wave through the etheric plane. At that moment, Johann was conducting a séance in Heidelberg for the family of the late Heinrich Wagner. The spirit of a recently deceased Chinese boy reached through the etheric plane, asking Johann to help his family, which was in danger in Chengdou. The shock wave was conducted through the child, then through Johann, killing everyone in the Wagner family.

While the Chinese government kept the B.P.R.D. out of Chengdou, the Bureau was able to investigate the fatal séance in Heidelberg. The agent on the scene, a psychic named Izar Hoffman, sensed a lingering spirit. Hoffman was surprised to

find the spirit to be lucid and focused, with none of the confusion that usually accompanies a violent death. It was Johann, who explained that he was not really dead—that his ectoplasmic form had somehow survived the Chengdou shock wave when his body was destroyed. He explained that he was not ready to move on, that he felt there was still work for him to do on earth. An incident in a Heidelberg cemetery roused Johann from the guilt and depression he'd felt over the Wagner family, and he accepted an offer from Hoffman—the German branch of the B.P.R.D. had been experimenting with an ectoplasm containment suit, and they found Johann the perfect test subject. Johann agreed, the test was successful, and, in early March, he traveled to the United States where he joined the B.P.R.D. as a field agent.

Whereas ectoplasm had once been his means to leave his body, now it *was* his body. This made him especially sensitive to psychic impressions. He could also extend out of his containment suit to create temporary physical forms for disembodied spirits, or to travel into the etheric plane, as long as he maintained contact with his suit. If separated from his suit for too long, his spirit could disperse into the atmosphere, and he'd be lost entirely.

His first field assignment with the B.P.R.D. was to retrieve Liz Sherman after her spirit had been stolen from the monastery in the Ural Mountains above the Arctic Circle. Going underground with Abe Sapien and Roger the Homunculus, Johann proved a valuable addition to the B.P.R.D., and formed a deep attachment to his fellow agents.

NOW PLEASE, SPEAK TO US. TELL US WHAT YOU ARE... HOW YOU CAME TO DIE HERE... AND WHAT HAS HAPPENED TO ELIZABETH SHERMAN.

The most surprising fact about Johann, from the moment he arrived at B.P.R.D. headquarters in Connecticut, was how at peace he seemed with his new situation, having no physical body. He took to his containment suit with ease, and had no trouble interacting with new people through the suit. When frog creatures destroyed that suit, Johann quickly got back to the mission at hand, temporarily inhabiting the body of a dead dog.

The first incident that did affect Johann came in 2004, after the B.P.R.D. moved its headquarters to a long-abandoned research center in Colorado. Within the first few days at the new headquarters, Johann began to exhibit bizarre behavior, the result of being possessed by the spirits of German scientists who had died at the facility years before. He allowed the scientists to act through him to defeat a Nazi who had been transformed into a giant insectlike creature from another dimension.

The biggest blow to Johann since his arrival at the B.P.R.D. was the death of Roger the Homunculus at the hands of the Black Flame. Roger was one of the first people Johann had bonded with after the Chengdou incident; despite the destruction of Roger's body, Johann was no more able to accept Roger's death than he'd been able to accept his own. He lashed out at his teammates for giving up on Roger, and then traveled into Roger's remains. There, Johann encountered Roger's spirit and tried to persuade him to come back to the world. But, unlike Johann, Roger felt his time on earth was finished, and Johann had no choice but to accept that and to say goodbye.

In 2007, Johann briefly found himself returned to corporeal life, with the aid of an engineered body retrieved from the hidden headquarters of the Oannes Society. He took advantage of his new body by overindulging in the pleasures of the flesh, neglecting his Bureau duties and alienating his colleagues. However, the body was destroyed in a fight with Captain Benjamin Daimio, the B.P.R.D.'s former field leader, transformed into a jaguar creature. Following the destruction of his body, Johann's ectoplasmic form was briefly possessed by the ghost of masked hero Lobster Johnson, who used Johann's ectoplasm to shoot the mysterious stranger attempting to control Liz Sherman's mind. Johann retained no memory of the possession, and he returned to his containment suit shortly after.

KARL RUPRECT KROENEN

L ittle is known about the early life of Professor Doctor Karl Ruprect Kroenen. Historical records indicate that he was born around 1880 in a small village south of Berlin. Kroenen always considered himself German, although his mother was a Norwegian heiress.

Kroenen became interested in science at an early age, conducting experiments freezing and thawing out living creatures while vacationing at his family's castle in Norway. He continued his experiments throughout his childhood. Kroenen later attended medical school, where he was a promising student with great surgical aptitude, but his interest in experimentation often took him away from his studies. He'd sometimes leave school for a year at a time to indulge in his independent projects. His focus was less on preserving life than on extending it beyond what others consider possible; he seemed to have shown little or no concern for the moral implications of his research.

In 1921, Kroenen met Herman von Klempt, a younger student at the school. Within four months, the two men had developed a fast friendship, built upon their unconventional theories and their private experiments transplanting body parts and reviving corpses. The friends fueled and fed off each other's energy, but it was an unequal relationship. In von Klempt, Kroenen had finally found a companion to share his work and his dreams of conquering death. Von Klempt, on the other hand, was uninterested in a confidant; he had attached himself to Kroenen in order to take advantage of Kroenen's family money and social connections. After graduation, the two professors of medicine expanded their focus to the study of electricity and mechanical engineering.

In September 1930, Kroenen was severely injured while testing an experimental power source. Von Klempt saved his life with a series of operations. The extent and nature of those operations is unknown, but Kroenen was never again seen without his face and body fully covered.

In 1935, Kroenen and von Klempt's work attracted the attention of Heinrich Himmler, who asked them to join his new German Occult Bureau. With the wealth of the Third Reich behind them, Kroenen and von Klempt dreamt of an army of super soldiers, and while they weren't able to achieve the goal, they never abandoned it.

In January 1936, an accidental explosion almost killed von Klempt. Kroenen worked with Leopold Kurtz, a brilliant young Occult Bureau scientist, to save von Klempt, but they were only able to preserve his head in a jar. While this enabled von Klempt to continue his work, Kroenen would always feel guilty for not being able to fully restore his friend, as von Klempt had saved Kroenen six years before.

In May 1937, von Klempt and Kroenen were hard at work on their super-soldier project in a basement lab underneath Hunte Castle, Austria, where the Nazi space program had been gearing up since 1932. Two months later, on a routine trip to Berlin, Kroenen met Himmler's mysterious Russian agent, Rasputin, who was recruiting Occult Bureau members for his Ragna Rok project, one of many Nazi doomsday plans prepared for the inevitable Second World War. Over the course of a few late nights drinking in Hans Ubler's nightclub, Kroenen sensed something special about Rasputin and signed on for Ragna Rok. Kroenen didn't like the idea of leaving von Klempt, and giving up their dream project at Hunte Castle. Rasputin had no interest in von Klempt, though, and von Klempt failed to see what his partner saw in Rasputin. Ultimately, Kroenen moved back to Germany with Rasputin, while von Klempt continued their work alone in Austria.

The Ragna Rok project would take over seven years to complete, with Kroenen spending the majority of that time working with Leopold Kurtz on the Ragna Rok Engine. On a rare break, he briefly returned to the family castle in Norway to set up a permanent cryogenic stasis chamber.

On December 23, 1944, on Tarmagant Island, the group put Kroenen and Kurtz's engine to the test as the last stage of the Ragna Rok project. The project was an apparent failure. Even so, Rasputin promised Kroenen, Kurtz, and Ilsa Haupstein that their faith would save them. He sent the three of them to the cryogenic chamber in Norway, where they could wait out the war's aftermath. They remained frozen until the moment of Rasputin's death at Cavendish Hall, in May 1994. Undeterred by the decades that had passed, Kurtz and Kroenen immediately began to plan a new army, based on Kroenen's earlier work with von Klempt, while awaiting a sign from Rasputin.

In 1995, Roderick Zinco, the C.E.O. of Zinco Laboratories, had pledged allegiance to Rasputin's ghost. Rasputin sent him to the castle in Norway in order to finance their Ragna Rok army. Once he had established his intentions, Zinco told the Nazis what had happened in the last fifty years, including the rumored fate of von Klempt. The head in the jar had fled to South America after the war, and continued his work in the jungles there. He was believed to have been killed by Hellboy in 1959, near Macapa.

Kroenen still felt guilty for having abandoned von Klempt to join Ragna Rok, and had Zinco make inquiries about his friend. Zinco recovered von Klempt's head, which Kroenen restored to life over Kurtz's objections. Kroenen tried to convince his revived friend of the great destiny that awaited them if they completed

Rasputin's Ragna Rok project. Von Klempt was scornful of Kroenen's allegiance to Ragna Rok, and told him to forget about Rasputin, claiming that *he* had a dozen half-finished projects hidden away in South America, any one of which would make them the most powerful men in the world. Kurtz, a devout follower of Rasputin, overheard von Klempt's treacherous remarks and attacked von Klempt with a wrench. In the confusion that followed, Kroenen fatally stabbed Kurtz in the heart.

Kroenen was horrified by what he had done, but he also realized that despite his guilt, he was a fool to try to get von Klempt to work with the others, and that in doing so, he himself had ruined everything. The ghost of Rasputin appeared and blamed the whole group for the project's failure. The castle was destroyed, and presumably Kroenen was destroyed with it.

KATE CORRIGAN

Eminent folklore and history scholar Katherine Corrigan was born in Oakland, California, in 1958. She attended the University of California at Berkeley, graduating with honors in 1980. Corrigan went on to the University of Bucharest, and, as part of her doctoral research, traveled throughout Europe to record peasants and villagers relating the myths and legends of their countries. She compiled the recordings into an oral history, still consulted as a primary text for specialized research in the occult fields.

In 1983, Corrigan published the first of her sixteen books, a study of werewolf trials in fifteenth-century France, and shortly thereafter she was offered an assistant professorship at New York University. At the same time, she began serving as an independent consultant to the B.P.R.D. Over the next ten years, Corrigan published over a dozen books, including a series on European witchcraft, each volume focusing on a particular country. The books were well received by her colleagues, and garnered favorable reviews in the academic press, but held little general appeal.

Corrigan met Hellboy in 1984, in the course of her work for the B.P.R.D. In 1985, they began a series of interviews, which she intended to turn into a book. The interviews continued over the next few years. During the course of the interviews, they became friends, and although the book was never published, Corrigan stayed in contact with Hellboy, who encouraged her to explore fieldwork, insisting, "There are some things you just can't learn from books." In 1994, she finally agreed, and saw her first ghost during an investigation into mass killings in the Balkan village of Griart. Though shaken by the experience, she was also thrilled to be working directly in the field she had researched so heavily. In 1998, she resigned her teaching position in order to join the B.P.R.D. as a full-time agent.

At first, Corrigan worked mainly at the central office as a consultant and researcher; in June 1999, she was promoted to assistant director of field operations. In 2002, Thomas Manning became the B.P.R.D.'s director, and Corrigan replaced him as director of field operations. When the infestation of frog creatures broke out in 2004, her position was given to Captain Benjamin Daimio, who had the necessary military background. Corrigan moved into the new Colorado headquarters, assuming the role of special liaison to the enhanced talent task force.

Her new position took the forty-six-year-old academic out of fieldwork for the most part, with the exception of a trip to France. After Roger the Homunculus was destroyed in 2005, Corrigan traveled to Ableben to recover a copy of *Flamma Reconditus*, or *The Secret Fire*, which was believed to contain the secrets of homunculus generation. The book had in fact been the basis of the work of Roger's creator, Edel Mischrasse. Corrigan was kidnapped by the book's current owner, the Marquis Adoet de Fabre, a five-hundred-year-old collector of rare occult artifacts. The Marquis offered to trade Corrigan's life for either Roger's remains or the living, breathing Abe Sapien. Corrigan's years in the field had at the very least made her resourceful: she thwarted Fabre's plan and managed to survive when Fabre was dragged into Hell by one of the creatures he'd collected.

LANGDON EVERETT CAUL

See also Abe Sapien, the Heliopic Brotherhood of Ra

Langdon Everett Caul was born on July 24, 1798, in Charlottesville, Virginia. He was the youngest son of a wealthy Virginia family that had made its fortune running trade ships up and down the East Coast and Canada. Though Caul himself did not grow up on a plantation, his family was close enough to the agrarian life of the South to be influenced by its manners. As a youth, Caul was expected to excel in the manly virtues, including horseback riding  and shooting. To his father's and brothers' disappointment, however, the young Caul preferred to spend his time growing mushrooms in the cellar or catching turtles at the river behind his family's estate.

When he was ten, Caul began to keep a journal, recording his observations of plant and animal life, writing personal thoughts, and occasionally composing poetry. In 1810, when Caul was twelve years old, his father discovered the journals and, dismayed by what he called his son's "silly bent," used the opportunity to convince Caul's mother that the child should be sent away to work on one of the family's ships, to "learn through difficulty the rights and responsibilities of men." Caul never completely forgave his father for sending him away.

The captain of that ship, a childless man named Edward Henry, took a liking to Caul. For the next seven years, Caul sailed with Henry during the trading seasons, and boarded with the captain and his wife for the rest of the year. The Henrys were happy to allow Caul to indulge his scientific inclinations, and he immersed himself in the study of biology and zoology, avidly following the evolutionary theories of French scientist Jean-Baptiste Lamarck.

In 1815, Captain Henry's wife became pregnant. Not wishing to overstay his welcome, Caul left the house and, with no place else to go, returned home for the first time since 1810. The years had not been kind to his family. Two of his brothers were dead; another had lost a leg to gangrene. Caul's father, now an old man, saw that the years away had indeed made a man out of his prodigal son. He tried to convince Caul to stay in Charlottesville and take over the family business, but Caul, who had fallen in love with life at sea and still hoped to pursue his scientific interests, refused.

In the summer of 1816, Caul once again left Virginia to travel up and down the eastern seaboard. The details of his life during these months are unknown, but early in 1817, he returned to the home of his benefactor, Captain Henry, only to discover that Henry's wife had died in childbirth and the captain himself had been lost at sea. Bereft of the only real family he had known, and his last ties to land, Caul traveled to New York and signed on as a deckhand on the ship of British whaler Elihu Cavendish.

Cavendish was a different sort of captain than Henry had been: tough, exacting, and often cruel. On the ship, he kept mostly to himself, and in port he would often disappear in the company of strange-looking men, returning with peculiar packages whose contents he shared with no one. His sailors respected his command but whispered of dealings with black magic.

Sensing he could rise through the ranks on Cavendish's ship if he kept quiet and respected Cavendish's privacy, Caul gradually gained the captain's limited trust. "I do not think he likes me," Caul wrote in his journal, "but, with so many men to hate, neutrality is the same as affection." Within only a few years, Caul rose rapidly from deckhand to Captain Cavendish's personal secretary. Caul would ultimately sail under Cavendish for sixteen years, and although their relationship was never a friendship of equals, Cavendish became fond of Caul, telling him stories—usually while drunk—of his adventures at sea.

In March 1833, Cavendish, more drunk than usual, finally took Caul into his confidence and showed the secretary the collection of strange charms and carvings that Cavendish had amassed over the years. He also showed Caul his most treasured and secret possession—a parchment inscribed with text neither of them could read—all the while rambling about strange creatures buried in the earth "since the beginning of time," secret ceremonies he had witnessed, and a race older than man, whose secrets were buried somewhere in the Arctic.

Although Caul found most of Cavendish's ramblings difficult to believe, he was fascinated by the idea of a prehuman race, and for several nights had vivid dreams of fantastic cities lost beneath the sea and buried under the polar ice. Unfortunately, he found that he couldn't discuss the matter further: Cavendish clearly thought that he had told his secretary too much. The captain became increasingly paranoid and volatile, on several occasions even accusing Caul of snooping around his cabin. Caul denied the (false) charges and stayed out of the captain's way until June 1833, when Cavendish's ship docked on the coast of England, and Caul disembarked with no plans to return.

Caul decided not to go back to sea; rather, he remained in England, pursuing private scientific investigations in order to "better understand the workings of this vast stage we call the world." In London, he befriended British doctor and fossil hunter Gideon Mantell (1790–1852), as well as other notable scientists involved in the discovery and reconstruction of extinct species. He was fascinated by the idea of evolution: that all life on Earth developed not from God, but from the ocean.

Caul's research caught the eye of Dr. Norman Netaunt, an elder of the Oannes Society, who invited Caul to a Society meeting outside of Oxford in July 1834. Since its split from the more prominent Heliopic Brotherhood of Ra, the Oannes Society had remained a small and highly exclusive group dedicated to the exploration of the lost civilizations and prehuman life forms that they believed to exist beneath the sea. "I sit with trembling hand," Caul wrote in his journal that night. "After thirty-six years of what surely must have been my exile, I feel (I hope!) that in the Oannes Society, I have found my brothers and my home." He was officially initiated into the society the following month, in Paris.

Caul was not disappointed. The Oannes Society, though small, was well funded by a few of its wealthiest members and had access to the most advanced scientific equipment of the day. For the next eight years, Caul traveled widely with his newfound brothers, testing the bounds of both science and technology. When his father died in 1845—leaving Caul his entire estate—Caul sold off the family business and other assets and donated most of the money to the Oannes Society to finance further expeditions.

In the early 1850s, the Oannes Society decided that the time had come for them to establish a base of operations in America, and in 1853, Caul traveled to Littleport, Rhode Island, with a set of architectural plans drafted by the Oannes Society. The Littleport house took eight years and the remainder of Caul's inheritance to complete, and all of the construction was done by foreign—mainly French—workers.

During this time, Caul oversaw the construction of the house while taking periodic trips to England, France, and Australia on Oannes Society business. On one such trip, in 1859, Caul and several other Society members traveled to London to witness the unrolling of a living Egyptian mummy, a display that particularly captured Caul's imagination. "If there has been any question among the nay-sayers," Caul wrote in a letter to an Oannes brother, "this proves it. Do not doubt that the Ancients held secrets that dwarf our Modern Sciences."

In 1861, work on Caul's house was completed, and he decided it was time for him to marry. Because of his wealth, he was perceived as a desirable—if eccentric—catch by many local families, and after a brief formal courtship, he married Edith Howard, a beautiful but highly sensitive girl from Littleport.

However, marriage did little to settle Caul, nor did it shift his first allegiance from the Oannes Society. In letters to her family, Edith complained that between his scientific investigations, his continual travel, and the frequent visits from "strange, foreign gentlemen," she scarcely saw her husband; further letters described "unnatural experiments" and mysterious locked rooms. Concerned by her "wild imaginings," Edith's family sent a doctor to evaluate her; he diagnosed her with mild hysteria, which was to be treated with a strict course of lithium and rest. Caul stayed slightly closer to home, but his attention was soon drawn elsewhere: in

1865, following a flurry of letters, he left home once again, telling his wife only that he would return for good after this expedition. However, after Caul had been gone for little more than a month, Edith threw herself into the sea. Her body was never recovered.

Caul never learned of his wife's death. Days before, on a dive to investigate undersea ruins, Caul had discovered an egglike artifact, which he subsequently transported to one of the society's secret laboratories, in a sub-basement of St. Trinian's Hospital in Washington, D.C.

On April 9, 1865, Caul and four of his society brothers attempted to make contact with the entity inside the egg, via a complex ritual. All five men entered a trancelike state, and four began unconsciously writing in a nonhuman language, while Caul himself was briefly possessed by the entity within the egg. A second later, Caul and

the others awoke from their trance, and the egg crumbled to dust. At that moment, the ghost of Abe Sapien, Caul's future self, entered the chamber and merged with Caul, who fell unconscious.

Over the next few days, the still-unconscious Caul began to transform into an amphibious fish-man. His companions dubbed him "Icthyo Sapien" and moved him to a tank of water for further study. However, on April 14, 1865, they were forced to flee America—likely because of connections between the Oannes Society and President Lincoln's assassination. They sealed the basement room with Caul's tank inside, promising to return "when it is safe." On April 17, 1865, neighbors observed several "foreign-looking" men entering Caul's house and removing boxes of his belongings. Edith Howard's family tried to claim Caul's property, but Caul's will left his entire estate to Alexandre Gasquet, a French weapons manufacturer, who left the house vacant.

LEOPOLD KURTZ

Leopold Kurtz was born in the countryside south of Berlin to a middle-class family on October 11, 1915. Kurtz was a dwarf, but more than made up for his size with his talent for the sciences. He graduated from secondary school two years ahead of his class, and in 1930 he enrolled at Friedrich Wilhelms Universität in Berlin, then the center of cutting-edge scientific research in Europe. At the university, Kurtz distinguished himself with his academic rigor and his seriousness of purpose. He graduated when he was eighteen years old, now a full four years ahead of his peers.

In Berlin, Kurtz expanded his interests from the strictly scientific to the fields of occult theory and emerging ideas about alternate energy sources. In 1934, he met Professor Doctor Karl Ruprect Kroenen and Professor Doctor Herman von Klempt, two of the most brilliant scientific minds in Berlin. The three began to work together closely, and Kroenen in particular took to the young Kurtz, nicknaming him "Little Bulldog."

In July 1935, Kurtz was invited to join Heinrich Himmler's new Occult Bureau, along with Drs. Kroenen and von Klempt. An ambitious twenty-year-old, Kurtz saw the Bureau as a means to fund his scientific research. A year into his work with the Occult Bureau, he helped to save the life of Dr. von Klempt, who was nearly killed when one of his own experiments with Dr. Kroenen resulted in an explosion. Kurtz was able to save von Klempt by keeping his head alive—and completely functional—in a jar of fluid.

Two years after Kurtz joined the Occult Bureau, he was recruited by Rasputin, who found the diminutive genius to be one of the most rational of Hitler's scientists. Kurtz and Kroenen were assigned to help develop Rasputin's Ragna Rok Engine, one of the many doomsday projects that would be initiated in the closing days of World War II. Of Kurtz's colleagues, Ilsa Haupstein had her relationship with the vampire Giurescu, and Kroenen had his friendship with von Klempt, but Kurtz became entirely devoted to Rasputin, concentrating only on pleasing his new mentor.

On December 23, 1944, Rasputin used the Ragna Rok Engine to try to free the Ogdru Jahad from their crystal prisons. After the engine apparently failed, Kurtz, Haupstein, and Kroenen placed themselves in cryogenic stasis in Kroenen's castle in Norway. They remained in stasis for fifty years.

When they woke in May 1994—at the moment of Rasputin's death at Cavendish Hall—Kroenen convinced Kurtz to concentrate on the development of a super-soldier army, updating a project that Kroenen and von Klempt had planned, now influenced by Rasputin's Ragna Rok project. They aimed to create a Ragna Rok army of half-man, half-machine soldiers and turn it loose upon the world, triggering an earth-changing plague and famine. The scientists thought this would result in enough death to awaken the Ogdru Jahad and allow them to return to earth, fulfilling Rasputin's thwarted vision.

In 1995, Roderick Zinco, the C.E.O. of Zinco Laboratories, arrived at the castle in Norway, claiming that Rasputin's ghost had appeared to him. The scientists used Zinco's money to fund the construction of their apocalypse army. While Kurtz continued to work on the army, Ilsa Haupstein traveled to retrieve the vampire Vladimir Giurescu, and Kroenen sent Zinco's men to recover the head of Professor von Klempt.

Kroenen recovered von Klempt's head and restored it to life, but the head had never respected Rasputin or the Ragna Rok project. In 1996, Kurtz overheard von Klempt trying to turn Kroenen from Rasputin's instructions. Kurtz attacked von Klempt with a wrench. Kroenen tried to stop Kurtz from destroying von Klempt's head, and fatally stabbed Kurtz. Rasputin returned to find his plans in ruins, and the castle was destroyed, presumably killing all inside.

THE LOBSTER (A.K.A. LOBSTER JOHNSON)

The true identity of the masked crime fighter known as The Lobster has never been determined, although the date of his first appearance can be pinpointed with some certainty: in February 1934, the body of Donny "Mints" Parker, a two-bit gangster, was discovered backstage at the Alvin Theater, with a claw-shaped symbol seared into his forehead. For the next four years, The Lobster seemed to wage a one-man war on gangs, with over a hundred (by some counts, as many as 250) gang-related victims confirmed between 1932 and 1938, including

such figures as Zuco Banana, Skinny Joe Lincoln, and Victor "Vicky the Fish" Cipriani. Whether the killings were the work of one man, an organized team, or scattered copycats was never determined, but the legend of The Lobster was burned into America's consciousness.

In the late 1930s, The Lobster's focus apparently shifted from domestic crime to international affairs, and his claw marks appeared on the foreheads of the Polish husband-and-wife spy team Ivan and Vana Krapowsky and the Brazilian saboteur Little Cheen. In 1939, a widely circulated rumor held that The Lobster had been recruited by the U.S. Army to defend the home front against the Nazis. If this is true, The Lobster's patriotism may have cost the crime fighter his life: there have been credible claims that The Lobster was killed in 1939 on a top-secret army expedition to Hunte Castle in Austria. (There were no reports of Lobster victims after that year, a fact which lent credence to

the rumormongers' claim that The Lobster had died.) However, the rumors are impossible to confirm, as the United States government has consistently denied the existence of The Lobster, as well as his involvement in any U.S. Army operations.

Dead or alive, The Lobster continued to capture the public's imagination throughout the Second World War. In 1940, aspiring writer and former police detective Norvell Cooper, who claimed to have met and worked alongside The Lobster on several occasions, published a series of short Lobster stories in *Weird Detective* and *The Lobster Pulp Magazine*, giving The Lobster the fictional alter ego of wheelchair-bound millionaire Walter Johnson. Cooper completed a total of thirteen Lobster stories before *Weird Detective* went bankrupt and ceased publication in February 1942. Before the end of that year, The Lobster resurfaced in a comic book and radio serial, and remained popular throughout the war years, although the comic book went out of print in 1946.

In 1945, Republic Pictures released two Lobster serials, *The Phantom Jungle* and *The Legion of Death*, both starring actor Vic Williams in the main role, and both universally panned. With the failure of the films, The Lobster began to fade from American public consciousness. In 1951, Mexican director Eduardo Fernandez wrote and produced a string of wildly popular low-budget horror movies about

"Lobster Johnson" (the last name was borrowed from The Lobster's fictional alter ego in Cooper's stories). The Fernandez movies were so bizarre that some conspiracy theorists have hypothesized that the U.S. government bankrolled them in order to remove any lingering credibility from the legend of The Lobster.

In recent years, the ghost of The Lobster has been sighted several times: at the ruins of Hunte Castle, in February 2001; and in Alabama, in July 2003, with a ghost train he had

apparently failed to save from a Nazi saboteur. In September 2006, the ghost briefly possessed the ectoplasmic form of B.P.R.D. agent Johann Kraus and fired spectral bullets from his gun before disappearing.

THE MIRACLE BOY

On June 17, 1984, Humbert T. Jones was born in Marnet, West Virginia, to single mother Edna Jones. Nine years later, Jones made local news headlines as the Miracle Boy, a child who could heal with his touch.

Young Jones had been healing animals in secret for years, but he didn't catch the attention of the media until he healed the broken arm of a classmate who had fallen from the roof of the school. Once the story was reported, Jones's hometown was flooded with miracle seekers. In the next year, Jones performed sixteen public healings, all with empirically documented results.

On April 5, 1994, when Jones was ten years old, he fell into a trancelike coma. He awoke thirty-six days later, at the same moment that Abe Sapien, possessed by the spirit of Elihu Cavendish, harpooned Rasputin at Cavendish Hall. At the moment of Jones's awakening, several doctors witnessed a small wound appear in Jones's chest. The wound bled for the next hour or so, then disappeared without a trace.

In the days and weeks that followed, Jones refused to grant any interviews or perform public miracles, and the residents of Marnet began to lose interest in their erstwhile Miracle Boy. He began to withdraw more and more into his own private world. On occasion, he would return to his trancelike state and be visited by visions that he was later unable to explain. At the same time, Jones began to age at an accelerated rate, passing through puberty and into adulthood in a matter of months. This rapid aging continued until his death.

In 1997, Jones left Marnet. His activities for the next three years remained unknown, but in 2000, he surfaced in Crab Point, Michigan, where he founded the New Temple of Mysteries. Even then, Jones stayed out of the spotlight, quietly building his congregation, impressing the locals and gaining parishioners through displays of his healing powers. He promised his parishioners that "the new age of the Dragon" was coming and that his followers would be reborn as "the first of a New Race of Men."

One of the first and most loyal members of the New Church of Mysteries was Professor Irwin Derby, a local biologist on administrative leave from his university post. In the summer of 2004, Jones sent Professor Derby to kill Doctor Arnold Platt, a B.P.R.D. scientist supervising the study of a spore found at Cavendish Hall. Though Platt did not know it at the time, the spore he was cultivating was in fact the ancient creature Sadu-Hem, one of the Ogdru Hem. Derby murdered Platt, Sadu-Hem possessed Derby, and Jones's plan was realized: Sadu-Hem could now travel in the guise of a man, transforming believers into frog creatures—the New Race of Men Jones had foretold.

The B.P.R.D. tracked Professor Derby back to Crab Point, where they discovered the prematurely aged Miracle Boy presiding over a congregation full of frog creatures, worshiping Sadu-Hem. During the fight that followed, Jones speared B.P.R.D. agent Abe Sapien through the chest, fulfilling the prophecy that Rasputin's ghost had made years earlier in Romania—that Abe would die as Rasputin had died, "and the hands on the spear shaft will belong to another, but the heart that drives them will be mine."

Though wounded, Abe was still able to shoot Jones three times, once in the shoulder and twice in the chest. The injured Jones claimed that he had been chosen upon Rasputin's death to complete the work Rasputin had started, then walked into the burning forest. To this day, no physical evidence of his death has been found, although it is presumed that he burned to death or died of his gunshot injuries.

THE OGDRU JAHAD
AND OGDRU HEM

In the beginning, God created spirits, and many of these were sent to watch over the newly formed earth. They were to observe the slow emergence of life from its newborn oceans. For some of the watchers, however, the process proved too slow. They became restless.

One day, a watcher spirit named Anum dared to raise his right hand to "take fire out of the air and with it fashion out of the mud the Dragon, Ogdru Jahad." The Ogdru Jahad was in fact not one, but seven gigantic creatures. Some sources claim that the watchers intended them to be servants. Others believe that the creatures were intended to be the progenitors of all life on earth, a shortcut through the slow process of natural evolution.

The watchers gathered around the Ogdru Jahad and "set their seals upon them," naming them Amon-Jahad, Adad-Jahad, Namrat-Jahad, Irra-Jahad, Nunn-Jahad,

Belili-Jahad, and Nergal-Jahad. Anum breathed the stolen fire into the creatures, but they remained lifeless husks.

When night came, Ershkigal, the darkness, looked down on the Ogdru Jahad and entered into them, endowing them with function and purpose. In the morning they gave birth to the 369 Ogdru Hem—the first living creatures on Earth.

The watchers were horrified when they saw the Ogdru Hem, understanding at once that their creations had been corrupted by darkness and chaos. They had created the very thing they had been sent to guard against.

To try to right their mistake, the watchers waged war against the Ogdru Hem. The struggle lasted 10,000 years, and the watchers found that they could not destroy the Ogdru Hem completely. Even when the bodies of the Ogdru Hem were destroyed, their spirits remained. These spirits, roughly two-thirds of the Ogdru Hem, the watchers "cast out on the wind." The rest were entombed in the earth and under the sea, where they remain, still alive and waiting for the time when they will be set free, when those trapped in the air will manifest in new bodies, and they will reclaim the earth.

Even after the watchers had vanquished the Ogdru Hem, the seven Ogdru Jahad remained, and the watchers could not destroy them. The watchers appealed to Anum, who used the last of the fire he had stolen to imprison the Ogdru Jahad in crystal-like shells, which he hurled into the Abyss.

Although the Ogdru Hem and the Ogdru Jahad had been imprisoned, they were far from impotent. In Hyperborea, in the temple of Gorinium, priests prayed night and day for protection from the Beast Jahad, who "would give the world back to chaos." When the Black Goddess, Heca-Emem-Ra (Hecate) profaned that temple, she caused Sadu-Hem, one of the disembodied Ogdru Hem, to be reborn. Sadu-Hem grew from the spilled blood of murdered priests and remained in the temple until 1993 A.D.

Prehistoric humans both worshiped and feared the Ogdru Hem, whom they usually characterized as demons, gods, or spirits of the earth. They performed rituals, made sacrifices, shaped idols, and built primitive temples at the places where the Ogdru Hem slept beneath the earth.

Some prehistoric shamans were believed to have been able to communicate with the disembodied Ogdru Hem spirits, and early worshipers believed that the lesser Ogdru Hem could possess both humans and animals to create new bodies for themselves. There is some archaeological evidence of battles between early humans and these Ogdru Hem creations, and the bones discovered by B.P.R.D. agents in Evanston, Illinois, in 1974, are believed to have been the remains of one of these.

In 1525, on an island off the coast of Portugal, a former Catholic priest devoted to the worship of the Ogdru Jahad was killed by soldiers of the Inquisition. Just as Sadu-Hem had risen from the blood of the priests killed at Gorinium, another of the disembodied Ogdru Hem, Urgo-Hem, was reborn out of the priest's spilled blood.

The earliest recorded direct contact between humans and the Ogdru Jahad took place almost four centuries later. In 1916, the Russian sorcerer and political magnate Rasputin was poisoned, beaten, shot, and thrown into the frozen Neva River. At the moment of his death, Rasputin heard the voice of the Dragon and pledged himself to its service, to help the Ogdru Jahad "usher in a new world and a New Race of Men." Rasputin's chance came in 1937, when Heinrich Himmler recruited him to Himmler's newly established Sonnenrad Society, the Nazi Occult Bureau. There, Rasputin set in motion a project he called Ragna Rok: the creation of a mystical engine to free the Ogdru Jahad from their crystal prison in the Abyss. The engine took years to complete but was finally activated on Tarmagant Island, off the coast of Scotland, in December of 1944. There were no apparent results (although, unknown to Rasputin and his allies, Hellboy had appeared in the ruins of a church in East Bromwich, England, at the moment the engine was activated), and the Nazis deemed the project a failure.

While Rasputin was initiating the construction of the Ragna Rok Engine in 1937, another group of Nazis at Hunte Castle in Austria made contact with a disembodied Ogdru Hem. In 1939, they launched a capsule containing the specially prepared body of Nazi scientist Ernst Oeming into space; they hoped that Oeming's body would serve as a vessel for the spirit they had contacted. In 2001, the capsule finally returned to Hunte Castle, where it emitted a gas that transformed all nearby humans into frog creatures. The body of Ernst Oeming had become a vessel for the Ogdru Hem known as the Conqueror Worm, which was eventually destroyed by Roger the Homunculus, aided by Hellboy and the ghost of 1930s adventurer Lobster Johnson.

The Conqueror Worm incident was far from Hellboy's first experience with the Ogdru Hem. In March 1965, at the French abbey of La Noe, he had battled a strange ectoplasmic emanation that was later identified as one of the Ogdru Hem. In 1979, Hellboy tried to save the medium Mr. Tod from another ectoplasmic Ogdru Hem manifestation. Although he was unable to save Mr. Tod, Hellboy managed to prevent the creature from assuming physical form, and drove it "back to wherever it came from" with a burning arbutus plant.

In 1993, the Cavendish Arctic expedition discovered the Hyperborean Temple at Gorinium. Inside, they found and woke Sadu-Hem. Upon waking, Sadu-Hem transformed the Cavendish brothers and Sven Olafsen into frog creatures. With Sadu-Hem sat Rasputin, whom the Ogdru Jahad had called to the temple in 1945, in the wake of the failure of the Ragna Rok project. Rasputin had remained there ever since, in meditative communion with Sadu-Hem and, through him, the Ogdru Jahad.

After being jarred from his trance by the Cavendish expedition, Rasputin brought Sadu-Hem to Cavendish Hall in upstate New York, where he attempted to channel Liz Sherman's pyrokinetic powers, combined with his own arcane powers, through Sadu-Hem and into the Abyss. If he had been successful, the power would have broken the crystal prison the watchers had created for the Ogdru Jahad, setting them free. Rasputin believed that once they were free, the Ogdru Jahad would bring about Ragna Rok.

Even though Hellboy was at Cavendish Hall—Rasputin had called him to "stand beside me at Ragna Rok, to command the power I shall unleash upon the world"—it was Abe Sapien who finally killed Rasputin by throwing a spear through his chest. Liz Sherman's fire destroyed Sadu-Hem, and, though Rasputin was able to crack one of the Ogdru Jahad prisons, it was not enough to wake them or set them free. It was generally assumed that, with Rasputin's death and the destruction of Sadu-Hem, the matter was closed.

In 2004, B.P.R.D. investigators discovered a fungus spore during a routine sweep of the ruins of Cavendish Hall. The spore, grown in the B.P.R.D. laboratory, was a new manifestation of Sadu-Hem.

At the moment of Rasputin's death at Cavendish Hall, the Ogdru Jahad had chosen a new servant: Humbert T. Jones, the West Virginia Miracle Boy. It was Jones who helped to free Sadu-Hem from the B.P.R.D. laboratory, after which Sadu-Hem took over a human body and was able to go about in the shape of a man, transforming believers into froglike creatures, the New Race of Men. During this time, Sadu-Hem transformed the entire population of Crab Point, Michigan, into frog creatures before it was stopped by the B.P.R.D.

According to Jones, the frog creatures would be "drawn to the secret places," and they would "remember the old songs and sing and pray until they cause the old gods [the Ogdru Hem] to wake." Liz Sherman's fire destroyed Sadu-Hem for the second time, and many of the frog creatures were killed as well. Some of the creatures escaped. In secret, they began to breed.

The B.P.R.D. continued to discover evidence of the frog creatures, who seemed to worship the Ogdru Hem through combinations of crude altars, carvings, and crypto-glyphs. On at least four more occasions, B.P.R.D. agents were killed by half-materialized Ogdru Hem spirits.

In 2006, the frog creatures succeeded in waking one of the buried Ogdru Hem, called Katha-Hem. Aided by the one-time C.E.O. of the Zinco Corporation, Landis Pope—now known as the Black Flame—Katha-Hem destroyed a large city and mutated several thousand humans into horrible creatures—not frog creatures, but something new—before Liz Sherman destroyed the massive Ogdru Hem by channeling her firepower through an ancient Hyperborean artifact. Although many of the frog creatures are presumed to have escaped, all efforts to track or locate them have been unsuccessful.

RASPUTIN

G rigori Yefimovich Rasputin was born in January 1869 in Pokrovskoe, Siberia. Raised in the Russian Orthodox Church, young Rasputin manifested healing powers and claimed to experience religious visions; these consisted mainly of Christian symbols, although he also saw images more commonly associated with pagan folklore, including the shape-shifting Leszi and the egg that held the soul of the devil Koshchei the Deathless.

When Rasputin was twenty, he left Pokrovskoe to seek answers about his emerging powers. He spent three months in the monastery at Verkhoture; soon after he left, the Virgin Mary came to him in a lucid vision. While at Verkhoture, he also became associated with the Khlysty sect of the Eastern Orthodox Church.

In 1895, Rasputin had a vision that he at first believed was a second visitation from the Virgin Mary. It was actually from the Baba Yaga, a figure from Russian folklore, who came to Rasputin and told him that he had been chosen as an "agent of change, father of a new millennium." Five years later, Baba Yaga visited Rasputin

again, this time in the flesh. Impressed by her presence and excited by her prophecies, Rasputin gave the Baba Yaga half of his soul to bury in the roots of Yggdrasil, the World Tree, for safekeeping.

Rasputin initially thought that the new millennium he was to usher in would come through political action. In the years immediately following his visitation from Baba Yaga, Rasputin used his healing abilities, which could control young Prince Alexei's hemophilia, to gain power and influence in the Russian court. However, Rasputin gained enemies as well as friends, and in 1916, he was assassinated by Prince Felix Yusupov. Rasputin was poisoned, beaten, shot, and finally thrown into the frozen Neva river, where, at the moment of his death, he heard the voice of the Dragon, Ogdru Jahad. Believing that he had been chosen to fulfill the destiny the Baba Yaga had spoken of,

Rasputin answered the Dragon's call and pledged himself to help usher in a new world and a New Race of Men.

Evading his political enemies, Rasputin fled Russia and wandered south through Europe, eventually arriving at the Italian hill town of Postignano. There, he settled into an abandoned house and maintained a low profile for a few years, living under an assumed name as a hermit and mystic. Believing he was simple minded, the villagers pitied him and provided him with food in exchange for light labor.

Little by little, Rasputin gained the villagers' confidence and began to preach about Ragna Rok—the destruction of this world and the rise of a new one from its ashes. He quickly established a small group of followers, and his reputation grew, leaking into the occult community and through the avenues of power, until it reached Heinrich Himmler, who was then actively recruiting for his Nazi Occult Bureau, the Sonnenrad Society. Rasputin interpreted Himmler's arrival as a sign from the Dragon and convinced Himmler that his Ragna Rok idea would help Germany win the war. Himmler invited Rasputin to join the Occult Bureau.

In July 1937, Rasputin traveled with Himmler to Germany, to meet with Hitler and the scientists of the Sonnenrad Society. Choosing the scientists he deemed most rational—Ilsa Haupstein, Professor Doctor Karl Ruprect Kroenen, and Leopold Kurtz—Rasputin cultivated a tight inner circle and began developing the Ragna Rok Engine. The engine would give Rasputin the power to direct his own energy into the Abyss, bringing about a "miracle" that would "assure Germany's victory and give Hitler power over all nations of the earth"; it was in fact intended to free the Ogdru Jahad from their prisons. After a few years, Rasputin took Ilsa Haupstein into his confidence, telling her about the dawn of the new age and the coming of the New Race of Men. She pledged herself to helping him, although he had never told her—or the other members of his inner circle—his true identity.

On December 23, 1944, Rasputin's Ragna Rok project reached its climax with the activation of the Ragna Rok Engine on Tarmagant Island, off the coast of Scotland. It was believed to be a failure by all but Rasputin, who, though he did not know about Hellboy's appearance, was confident that he had set in motion events that would lead to the waking of the Dragon, Ogdru Jahad.

Although the engine had apparently failed, Rasputin had seen a vision of "a child come from fire, reborn in fire," who would be the herald of his new age. He also saw the end for Hitler, and he instructed his followers to hide themselves until he sent them further instructions. In a moment of clarity, Ilsa Haupstein realized his true identity and she pledged herself to his service; Kurtz and Kroenen, who were still unaware of his true identity, also pledged their loyalty.

Rasputin returned to Germany to wait for a sign from the Dragon. When no sign came, he began to despair. Then, in May of 1945, he heard the Dragon calling to him, this time instructing him to go north, to the Arctic.

Rasputin left Germany immediately and made his way to the ruins of the Hyperborean temple Gorinium, where one of the 369 Ogdru Hem lay dormant. Rasputin discovered the unmoving figure of Sadu-Hem at the temple, and he placed himself in a trance at its base, sending his mind into the creature and, through it, into the Abyss. Rasputin remained in this state, communing with the Ogdru Hem, for forty-eight years.

Early in 1993, an expedition—including the three Cavendish brothers, the last descendents of Elihu Cavendish; Swedish climber Sven Olafsen; and B.P.R.D. founder Trevor Bruttenholm—discovered the temple where Rasputin sat in stasis. Bruttenholm touched Rasputin, and the moment of contact not only awakened Rasputin and Sadu-Hem, but also allowed Rasputin to see everything in Bruttenholm's mind—including the life and history of Hellboy, who had appeared at East Bromwich at the moment that Rasputin had activated the Ragna Rok Engine. Rasputin concluded that Hellboy was the key to freeing the Ogdru Jahad from their prisons.

Sadu-Hem transformed the Cavendish brothers and Olafsen into frog creatures, the first of a New Race of Men, and ate the rest of the exploration party. He allowed Trevor Bruttenholm to survive, using him as bait to trap Rasputin's ultimate quarry: Hellboy. Bruttenholm returned to New York, where he made contact with Hellboy and was subsequently killed by one of the transformed Cavendish brothers. In the meantime, Rasputin and Sadu-Hem sailed to America, up the Hudson River, then traveled through a secret underwater passage that led to the ancient temple below Cavendish Hall, where they waited for Hellboy to arrive.

Rasputin didn't know what role Hellboy would play in the awakening of the Ogdru Jahad; he had simply presumed that once Hellboy understood his destiny as Beast of the Apocalypse he would accept his fate and work with Rasputin to bring about Ragna Rok.

However, Hellboy didn't arrive at Cavendish Hall alone, but with B.P.R.D. agents Elizabeth Sherman and Abe Sapien. Rasputin immediately sensed Liz's tremendous power, and his attention quickly turned from Hellboy. Believing that Liz's power, combined with his own, would be enough to free the Dragon without Hellboy's help, Rasputin kidnapped Liz and succeeded in channeling their combined powers through Sadu-Hem into the Abyss. He had succeeded in cracking one of the Ogdru Jahad's prisons and might actually have freed the Dragon, had he not been interrupted by Abe Sapien, who, possessed by the spirit of Elihu Cavendish, stabbed Rasputin through the chest with a harpoon. At the exact moment of Rasputin's death, the Dragon abandoned him and chose a new agent of change—the young Humbert T. Jones, otherwise known as the West Virginia Miracle Boy.

At the same moment, Rasputin's followers—Ilsa Haupstein, Karl Ruprect Kroenen, and Leopold Kurtz—who had placed themselves in suspended animation in Kroenen's

Norwegian castle shortly after the surrender of the Nazi forces in May 1945, began to revive. As they returned to their projects and awaited instructions from their master, Rasputin's spirit was wandering "among the doomed spirits, those trapped in the upper air of this world," and into the Abyss, where he once again came into contact with the imprisoned Ogdru Jahad. Although they no longer responded to him, he remained as determined as ever to free them and bring about the New Age of Man.

In March 1996, Rasputin's ghost contacted billionaire Roderick Zinco, asking him to serve as his agent. Under Rasputin's orders, Zinco traveled to Kroenen's Norwegian castle, where he bankrolled the new Ragna Rok project under development by Kroenen and Kurtz. (The new project involved the creation of a half-mechanical, half-human army of 666 soldiers who would bring plague and famine to the earth, "so much death that the human race will be depopulated by two-thirds." The scientists believed that the massive scale of the destruction would cause the Dragon to "stir in its prison.")

Rasputin's new plans no longer required Hellboy. Instead, Rasputin planned to create a new Beast out of Ilsa Haupstein. His spirit visited Ilsa at the vampire Vladimir Giurescu's castle. There, Rasputin told her that she would need to be more than flesh and blood to stand beside him "in the teeth of the Ragna Rok storm." The Baba Yaga had given Rasputin an iron maiden, which he hoped to use to transform Ilsa into a more powerful being, just as Rasputin's own death had given him powers he had never imagined in life.

However, this effort was to fail as well. The iron maiden containing Ilsa's body was possessed by the goddess Hecate. Kroenen and Kurtz's army project ended in a bloody fight. Zinco accidentally blew up the Norwegian castle and the Ragna Rok army. With his plans in ruins, Rasputin's ghost traveled to the World Tree to recuperate from his failures, and to draw strength from the half of his soul that the Baba Yaga had buried there. The Baba Yaga suggested that Rasputin stay with her, but he was still intent on bringing about Ragna Rok.

Leaving the World Tree, Rasputin tried one more time to free the Dragon, this time enlisting the help of Herman von Klempt—a former Nazi scientist, now a living head in a jar. Rasputin had disliked von Klempt when they had met in Germany during the war, but with the rest of his followers dead, Rasputin had few other options. At Hunte Castle, he and von Klempt called Ernst Oeming's Nazi space capsule back to earth. The capsule now contained one of the disembodied Ogdru Hem. When the capsule was opened, it released a gas which transformed every human it touched into a frog creature. The frog creatures, in turn, would consume all mankind and wake the

Ogdru Jahad from their prison. However, this plan failed, foiled by Hellboy, Roger the Homunculus, and the ghost of masked hero Lobster Johnson, who had apparently died at Hunte Castle in 1939.

In the wake of this final defeat, Rasputin was visited by the Hecate-possessed iron maiden. Hecate mocked Rasputin for thinking he could free the Dragon without using Hellboy's right hand. Rasputin could not bring himself to admit that he was only a pawn of greater powers, and it's unclear whether he destroyed himself or was destroyed by Hecate. The last remaining fragment of his soul was retrieved by the Baba Yaga, who placed it in an acorn shell that she placed around her neck, "close to her heart forever."

In a battle against Hellboy, the Baba Yaga expended all of her power—and intended to use the last bit of Rasputin's soul to continue the fight. Her servant, Koku, prevented her from doing so, and dropped the acorn containing the soul remnant into the roots of the World Tree, where it was lost.

ROGER THE HOMUNCULUS

The homunculus who would eventually be known as Roger was created in 1533 by Edel Mischrasse, a German philosopher and alchemist. While a student in Wittenberg, Mischrasse had discovered a copy of *Flamma Reconditus*, or *The Secret Fire*, carefully hidden in the university library—he would later claim that an angel had led him to the book. *The Secret Fire* is a Greek translation of an Egyptian text written by Ini-Herit in 700 A.D., in the sunken city of Menouthis. Ini-Herit claimed to have deciphered a version of the Emerald Tablet (the legendary stone that fell from Lucifer's head when he was cast out of heaven) engraved by the magician Hermes Trismegisthus (Hermes Thrice-Great). The significance and the meaning of the tablet's thirteen lines have baffled mystics for centuries; Ini-Herit's version purports to be "a true record of the workings of the Universal Machine, of the nature and function of celestial bodies, the transmutation of metals, and the creation and reconstruction of living things."

Mischrasse used the text as a starting point to create his homunculi—artificial men grown in jars using certain roots, herbs, and bodily fluids. Mischrasse studied and experimented for three years, perfecting his formulas and successfully creating several small homunculi before completing his first man-sized homunculus in 1529. He kept this first homunculus a secret, in order to study it and improve his understanding of the science, but eventually his fear of religious authorities led him to poison the creature and throw it into a well.

Over the next thirty-six years, Mischrasse continued his work, constantly on the move for fear of discovery and prosecution. He established and then abandoned laboratories in remote areas of Eastern Europe. Four years after creating his first full-sized homunculus, Mischrasse created his second, the creature that would later be known as Roger, grown in a jar at Czege Castle in Romania. Unlike Michrasse's previous creation, this second homunculus was brought to life with a bolt of lightning directed through an iron rod placed in a hole in the creature's chest. For

three years, Mischrasse worked closely with his second homunculus, teaching it to read and to speak, but the electrical charge of the lightning slowly faded, and the creature eventually stopped moving.

Having treated this second homunculus more like a son, Mischrasse could not bring himself to destroy it, so he sealed the inert body in the Czege Castle laboratory before heading west again. Mischrasse was able to avoid the attention of the Inquisition until 1565, when he was arrested in the town of Albi, in France, and thrown into prison. During his arrest, he swallowed the key to a hidden box containing his notes and the locations of his abandoned laboratories. Mischrasse sat in jail for a year, waiting for a trial that would never come.

Meanwhile, his first man-sized homunculus had willed himself back to life, and went in search of his creator, eventually finding Michrasse in the French prison. Mischrasse told the homunculus the location of the locked box containing his notes, and the creature strangled his creator and took the key from Michrasse's stomach.

The homunculus traveled to Albi to recover Mischrasse's notes. Though he learned of the second homunculus's existence, he did not try to find him, concentrating instead on continuing his creator's work. Following Mischrasse's example, he set up a lab in the burnt ruins of the Capatineni Monastery in Romania. Locals already believed the monastery to be haunted, which allowed the homunculus the privacy he needed; the occasional noise and smell from his work only served to increase the fear of the locals. At the same time, in the sealed laboratory at Czege Castle, the

second homunculus waited in stasis, unable to move or to speak, but aware of the slow passage of time. He remained that way for more than four hundred years.

In March 1997, B.P.R.D. agents Liz Sherman, Bud Waller, and Sidney Leach discovered the Mischrasse laboratory at Czege Castle while searching for the vampire Vladimir Giurescu. When they saw Mischrasse's second homunculus, Liz was drawn to the apparently lifeless body lying on the table. The creature sensed the power within Liz, and knew that while she wanted to be rid of what she considered a curse, that same power could recharge him. He drew Liz to him, and she placed a finger in the

chest hole into which Mischrasse had once directed lightning. Only as she released all of her fire into the homunculus did he realize something Liz herself didn't know—that the fire was a living part of her, and that she wouldn't survive without it. Unfortunately, by then he couldn't stop himself. In a frenzied moment, Agent Waller saw that Liz couldn't break the connection between herself and the thing. Hoping that pain would jolt her away from the homunculus, Waller shot Liz in the arm. With the connection broken, although too late to make a difference, the homunculus lashed out and killed Waller.

Horrified and confused, the newly awakened homunculus fled from the laboratory. When he calmed down, he was wracked by guilt at having destroyed two lives. He spent the following week wandering hillsides at night, stealing chickens for food. Having no desire to hurt anyone, he was again guilt ridden at having to kill a dog that attacked him where he hid by day. Distant memories of Bible passages that Mischrasse had taught him twisted his guilt into a sort of religious passion, driving him to steal a large cross from a chapel and climb into the mountains, where he begged God to destroy him for his sins.

Instead, his elder brother found him. For the last four centuries, Mischrasse's first homunculus had been continuing their creator's work. The first homunculus had succeeded in creating smaller homunculi, which he used as servants. He'd put them to work robbing graves to provide the raw material for his "great work"—the creation of a giant body. The first homunculus invited his brother to join him in that body, to be one forever, never to be alone again—"to build, grow, climb, to crack wide the celestial vault and rake there for secret knowledge."

Still guilty over what he had done to Liz Sherman, the second homunculus rejected his brother's offer, despite his desire for some connection after centuries of being alone. The older brother took over the giant body by himself, and faced off against Hellboy, who had come to recover Liz's fire while she lay dying in a nearby hospital. When it looked like the giant was going to kill Hellboy, the second homunculus begged his brother for another chance, to become one with the giant. The giant swallowed him whole, but the second homunculus used Liz's stolen fire to melt the enormous body from within, thereby destroying the closest thing he had to family, while saving Hellboy. The second homunculus wanted only to be left alone now, away from mankind, but Hellboy convinced him that he had to give the stolen fire back to Liz.

While driving to the hospital, Hellboy named Mischrasse's second homunculus Roger. They arrived minutes after Liz had died, but Roger returned the firepower to her, shocking her back to life. Once again drained of energy, Roger appeared to be dead, and was returned to B.P.R.D. headquarters, where he was studied for several months by doctors Cobb and Roddell. Having learned everything they could from the outside, the doctors planned to dissect Roger. However, Abe Sapien, who had nearly suffered the same fate years earlier, snuck into the lab and rerouted the electrical system to shock Roger back to life. Abe burned out a large part of the Bureau's electrical system, but it was the least he could do after Roger had saved Liz.

The shock provided the initial jolt necessary to reanimate Roger, but it would not last. He proved himself an asset to the Bureau, an innocent spirit despite what had happened to Liz and Waller, and a good guy whom everyone liked. He was quick to learn and eager to fit in and to make up for the trouble he'd caused. His superior strength and durability put him in a category with Hellboy, whom he tried to model himself after. In November 2000, Roger was made an official B.P.R.D. agent. A generator was implanted in his chest as a permanent energy source to replace the hole that Mischrasse had designed to receive lightning. Unknown to Roger or his fellow agents, though, that generator contained an incendiary device large enough to destroy him should he ever get out of control again.

In February 2001, Roger joined Hellboy on a mission to Hunte Castle, to intercept a returning Nazi space capsule that had been sent up sixty-one years earlier. Before heading to the castle, Hellboy was given the detonator for Roger's bomb. Hellboy was outraged that the B.P.R.D. had put a bomb inside a fellow agent, but he was

forced to accept the situation. It never occurred to him that he might need to use the bomb.

At the castle, Roger encountered the ghost of the 1930s crime fighter The Lobster, as well as frog creatures and one of the 369 Ogdru Hem, a disembodied creature that had manifested as the Conqueror Worm. Roger shot electricity that he'd siphoned from the castle generators into the Conqueror Worm, destroying it, then sucked the disembodied creature's spirit into himself. With the spirit taking control of him, Roger begged Hellboy to detonate the bomb in his chest, to destroy him. When Hellboy refused, Roger threw himself down the side of the mountain. He was saved when the ghost of Lobster Johnson inserted an iron staff into his chest hole, which acted as a lightning rod to destroy the Ogdru Hem spirit inside him. Later, Roger was fitted with a new generator, this time without a bomb. Although he was restored, the bomb incident contributed to Hellboy's decision to quit the B.P.R.D.

While he missed the strong role model that he'd had in Hellboy, Roger continued to prove himself as an agent. Over the next four years, he traveled on B.P.R.D. missions with other agents, most notably the 2002 rescue of Liz Sherman from beneath the Ural Mountains. Bound together by that watershed mission, this team—Roger, Liz, Abe, and Johann—formed the tightest-functioning group the Bureau had ever known. Roger developed good relationships with all his fellow agents, but he maintained an especially close connection to Liz Sherman, from the time when she had brought him to life, and he, in turn, had brought her back. While in Venice in April 2003, Roger encountered Cloacina, the Roman goddess of sewers, and fell deeply in love, although he would never see her again.

In October 2004, the group dynamic changed again, when Captain Benjamin Daimio became the new commander of B.P.R.D. field operations. Daimio's forceful personality made a big impression on Roger, and, as the team dealt with the escalating frog-creature problem, Roger modeled himself after Daimio, starting to smoke cigars, and spouting military lingo that seemed out of character for a 450-year-old homunculus.

While cleaning out a nest of frog creatures in an abandoned steel works in Ontario, Canada, Roger encountered the Black Flame—actually Landis Pope, the head of Zinco Industries, posing as the updated incarnation of the World War II–era supervillain. Roger and several other agents were incinerated by the Black Flame, and Roger's body was petrified and shattered. The remains were recovered by the B.P.R.D. shortly thereafter.

Hoping to find a way to bring Roger back to life, agent Kate Corrigan went to France to obtain a copy of *The Secret Flame* from a rare-book dealer. The dealer turned out to be the 500-year-old Marquis Adoet de Fabre, who wanted Roger's

remains for his collection of occult objects. Kate defeated Fabre, but failed to get the book.

Johann, who had been most adamant in refusing to accept Roger's death, used his unique abilities to travel into Roger's burnt remains. He was surprised to find Roger at peace in a strange Italian garden, sitting under a statue of Cloacina. Johann, whose background was in conversing with spirits and sometimes helping to guide them into the afterlife, asked Roger why he lingered in the garden rather than going on. Roger explained that since he was never a human, there was nowhere for him to go on *to*, and that he liked it in the garden, a serene place of his own creation. "I'm happy here," he told Johann. "It's peaceful. No enemies I need to kill. I didn't like all that killing. I didn't like how easy it became for me."

Roger's one request of Johann was to be buried like a man, even though he knew he wasn't one. Johann of course agreed, although in order to protect the grave, the Bureau placed Roger's remains under a stone bearing a fake name, with a short inscription from the Book of Job:

"Great men are not always wise."

DR. THOMAS MANNING

Thomas Manning was born in 1946, in Somerville, Massachusetts. His father was a government employee and ex–army pilot; his mother, a homemaker. The second of three children, Thomas attended first a Catholic elementary school, then a public high school; at both, he received recognition as a top scholar and athlete. He participated in varsity athletics all four years of high school and was elected to homecoming court.

For college, Manning attended American University in Washington, D.C., where he earned a B.A. in international studies and physical education. After completing his undergraduate studies, he remained in Washington and received a Ph.D. in urban planning from Georgetown University. Although Manning's family and friends had expected him to enter the foreign service, Manning instead applied for a field position with the Bureau for Paranormal Research and Defense. His decision may have been related to the sudden death of his father, less than a month before Manning was due to receive his doctorate.

In 1980, after four years as a field agent, Manning was promoted to assistant to the director. After Trevor Bruttenholm resigned his directorship in 1982, Manning was assigned to assist with the interim director's transition and was promoted to director of field operations. For the next twenty years, Manning worked throughout the Bureau, gaining experience at all levels within the organization. In 2002, he became director of the B.P.R.D.

During his tenure as director, Manning has been responsible for the recruitment and training of dozens of B.P.R.D. agents, including Captain Benjamin Daimio. He also supervised field missions during the plague of frogs and the rise of the Black Flame. In addition, he oversaw the 2004 transition of B.P.R.D. headquarters to Colorado. While former and current B.P.R.D. employees have consistently characterized Manning as honest and fair, some of the longtime field agents have taken issue with his businesslike approach to the agency; his treatment of Roger—Manning authorized B.P.R.D. scientists to place an incendiary device inside the homunculus—was at least partly responsible for Hellboy's retirement from the B.P.R.D. in 2001.

TREVOR BRUTTENHOLM

Trevor Bruttenholm was born in Essex, England, on March 5, 1918. Trevor's father, a wealthy British barrister twenty years his wife's senior, fiercely regretted that his age prevented him from serving his country in the First World War.

When Bruttenholm was eight, his parents sent him to Oxford Preparatory School. Five years later, he became a student at Eton, an upper-class boarding school which four generations of Bruttenholm men had attended. As a gift for "going up" to Eton, Bruttenholm's uncle, an eccentric scholar who lived in the family estate in the north of the country, gave Bruttenholm an intricately carved obsidian box. The box became one of Bruttenholm's totems, and he carried it with him from Eton to Trinity College, Oxford, when he was eighteen.

Eton, and later Oxford, provided fertile ground for Bruttenholm's active imagination. At Eton, Bruttenholm joined the Ghost Club, a group that investigated rumors of hauntings and other supernatural occurrences. At Oxford, Bruttenholm and a few of his old Eton Ghost Club friends regularly snuck from their rooms to stand under the tree at the center of the New College quad where, it was rumored, they could observe witches walking the cloisters carrying bells. It was during his university years that Bruttenholm first became interested in the mystery surrounding the East Bromwich church where Hellboy would appear years later.

At the university, Bruttenholm studied politics, philosophy, and economics to please his father, who wanted him to take over the family law practice. However, his first love was literature. A dedicated disciple of the poetry of William Butler Yeats, Bruttenholm organized thirteen of his university friends to take a summer trip to see all of the circular towers in the British Isles. The journey was supposed to culminate in a visit to Yeats's home in County Sligo, Ireland. The group never made the crossing, however, and Yeats died before Bruttenholm could complete his literary pilgrimage.

Bruttenholm graduated from Oxford in 1938, on the cusp of World War II. Although most of his classmates became officers, Bruttenholm's father intervened, and Bruttenhom was offered a position in intelligence services headquartered in the north. Working for the army, he lived on the family estate with his eccentric uncle.

Bruttenholm's time with his uncle would prove more fruitful than Bruttenholm could have imagined. Set loose in his uncle's vast library, Bruttenholm followed his intellectual interests wherever they led. With his uncle as guide, Bruttenholm studied the writings of famous mystics and occult masters. The life of Sir Edward Grey, an occult detective and friend of his uncle's, became a particular point of interest for the young Bruttenholm. After hearing many tales of Grey's adventures, Bruttenholm decided to model his life and studies after Grey's. When Bruttenholm was twenty-two, his uncle recommended him for membership in the British Paranormal Society, and later took him to his first séance at Lady Cynthia Eden-Jones's cottage, an experience that marked the formal beginning of Bruttenholm's occult studies.

For the next six years, Bruttenholm focused all of his substantial energy and intellect on exploring the occult. With permission from the British army, he traveled throughout Allied territory, meeting with—among others—members of the Osiris Club and the Heliopic Brotherhood of Ra; he may even have been inducted into the Osiris Club during the early 1940s.

Bruttenholm became a leader in his field, an expert on spiritual mediums, folklore, fairies, and vampires. He used his expertise to advise Allied forces on occult matters throughout the war, and was awarded an honorary doctorate from Trinity College in recognition of his services to the Queen.

In 1944, Lady Cynthia Eden-Jones learned from her spirit guides that a cataclysmic event would soon take place at the East Bromwich church. Knowing of Bruttenholm's interest in the site, Lady Cynthia alerted him to the information. Bruttenholm, in turn, informed the war department, and eventually a patrol of U.S. troops, led by Sergeant George Whitman, joined Lady Cynthia, Bruttenholm, and noted U.S. occult scholar Malcolm Frost at East Bromwich. The group arrived at the ruins on December 21, 1944, two days before the date when Lady Cynthia's guides had predicted that the event was to occur.

Meanwhile, on a tiny island off the Scottish coast, Rasputin and members of the Nazi Sonnenrad Society were preparing to activate the Ragna Rok Engine to free the Ogdru Jahad from their prison in the Abyss. At 7:29 p.m. on December 23, at exactly the moment that Rasputin called upon the Dragon, a ball of flames manifested in the East Bromwich church. Eventually, the flames died down, revealing a small, red, demonlike creature.

Sensing that there was more to the creature than its demonic appearance suggested, Bruttenholm named it Hellboy. The Americans secretly transported Hellboy to a New Mexico air force base, and Bruttenholm accompanied him. There, with a group of noted American occult experts and the support of the U.S. government, Bruttenholm founded the Bureau for Paranormal Research and Defense. The Bureau's stated purpose was the "continuing study and investigation of the creature known as 'Hellboy' and Nazi occult activities, particularly those related to the Ragna Rok project." Bruttenholm served as the B.P.R.D.'s first director.

At the same time, Bruttenholm continued to work closely with Hellboy. Bruttenholm's official notes from that period remain classified, but letters to his uncle show Bruttenholm's curiosity about and appreciation of Hellboy as a research subject rapidly developing into active affection. Instead of treating him like a freak or a dangerous experiment, Bruttenholm began to treat Hellboy like a human child, and, in 1946, he officially adopted Hellboy. Following the adoption, the pair took several trips together, and Bruttenholm helped Hellboy through the difficult transition from the New Mexico air force base to the new B.P.R.D. headquarters in Fairfield, Connecticut, in 1947.

For six years—from 1946 to 1952—Bruttenholm divided his time between leading field operations (including the discovery and neutralization of the remains of the Nazi doomsday project Vampir Sturm) and tending to the growing Hellboy at B.P.R.D. headquarters. He frequently traveled to Washington to lobby for funding and government support for the Bureau.

Partly because of Bruttenholm's political efforts, the United Nations granted Hellboy honorary human status on August 6, 1952. A week later, Bruttenholm promoted Hellboy to B.P.R.D. field agent and took him on a two-month trip— part celebration and part training—through the United States and Canada. The following year, the two traveled to the British Isles, where Bruttenholm passed on his love of and fascination with Britain's mysteries and landscape. Both would later look back on this trip as the happiest time of their lives. After the trip, Bruttenholm reluctantly returned to his administrative duties at B.P.R.D. headquarters and Hellboy began spending more time away from headquarters, working in the field.

In 1958, Bruttenholm received word of his uncle's death. His responsibilities as B.P.R.D. director prevented him from traveling to England for the funeral, and he began to reevaluate his role within the Bureau. His tenure as director had been extremely successful—his accomplishments had included the growth of the Bureau from five to fifty agents, the establishment of permanent headquarters in Connecticut, and the official recognition of the Bureau's work by the United Nations. In addition, Bruttenholm had instituted many of the practices that had contributed

to the B.P.R.D.'s success, including equipping every agent with a homing beacon, insisting on regular physical examinations, and mandating periodic breaks from fieldwork. But despite his successes as a leader, Bruttenholm's real interest was in the field, and in September of 1958, he resigned his directorship, remaining with the Bureau as an advisor and sometime field agent. This not only allowed Bruttenholm to return to his first and greatest love—occult investigation— but also gave him the opportunity to spend more time with Hellboy. The pair frequently worked together on assignments, although Bruttenholm was later pleased to see Hellboy develop close friendships with fellow B.P.R.D. agents Liz Sherman and Abe Sapien.

However, in 1979, Bruttenholm and Hellboy's relationship was put to the test: Hellboy, on an assignment in London, met and fell in love with Anastasia Bransfield, a British archeologist. Suddenly, Bruttenholm was confronted with the heart-wrenching realization that Hellboy was no longer a child, but he could not bring himself to allow Hellboy the autonomy he needed as an adult. He expressed constant disapproval of the relationship, blaming Bransfield for Hellboy's growing distraction from his work. Hellboy broke off his romance with Bransfield in 1981 and returned to the B.P.R.D., but his relationship with Bruttenholm was never the same.

As Bruttenholm aged, he became increasingly engaged in private research involving the ancient Lemurian language (which he had taught Hellboy years before). In the course of this research, Bruttenholm met and befriended the descendents of Elihu Cavendish, and, in 1992, the Cavendish brothers asked him to join them on an expedition to the Arctic. In November of that year, Bruttenholm said goodbye to Hellboy and set sail with the Cavendish Expedition. Shortly after the party left Bull Harbor, Bruttenholm's B.P.R.D. homing signal went dead. Six months later, the party was given up for lost.

In May 1994, Bruttenholm suddenly resurfaced and summoned Hellboy to his Brooklyn Park home. Bruttenholm could only remember bits and pieces of what had happened in the Arctic, but he told Hellboy about a Hyperborean temple at the top of the world and a mysterious figure seated at the base of a gigantic idol inside the temple. In the middle of their conversation, a rain of frogs began to fall outside Bruttenholm's window. Bruttenholm ran from the room in a panic

and was killed by a frog creature—
actually one of the transformed Cavendish brothers. Bruttenholm was
buried in Essex, England, not far from
the house where he was born. Shortly
thereafter, B.P.R.D. agents found a
carved obsidian box hidden in his
closet. Inscribed with the words "Here,
and Beyond," the box contained a will
that named Hellboy as Bruttenholm's
sole heir.

VLADIMIR GIURESCU

In 1492, while traveling in Greece, Mihail Giurescu, a Romanian nobleman with a noted interest in the occult, purchased the petrified body of the goddess Hecate from two fishermen. Upon his return to Romania, Mihail built a temple to Hecate at Castle Giurescu, with a secret subterranean chamber where he revived and housed the goddess.

There are no records of Mihail Giurescu ever marrying, but he apparently carried on a longstanding affair with a peasant from a nearby village. When his lover gave birth to a boy on December 12, 1495, Mihail Giurescu took the child, cutting off all communication with the mother, and possibly even arranging for her execution; regardless, young Vladimir grew up believing that she had died.

When Vladimir was twelve years old, his father invited him to enter the temple of Hecate. During that visit—a rite of passage for the young nobleman—Mihail introduced Vladimir to the ceremonies and ritual sacrifices with which he was to worship the goddess.

When he was eighteen, Vladimir was thrown from the back of his favorite horse and tumbled into an icy river. It took hours for his father's servants to find his body and chop it free of the ice. Mihail placed the frozen corpse on the steps of Hecate's

temple and sacrificed thirty-two dogs and half again as many servants during a three-day blood ritual. Three days after the ritual ended, Hecate returned Vladimir to life, giving the boy a piece of her spirit, turning him into a vampire.

From that day forward, Mihail declared Castle Giurescu and the area surrounding it to be under the rule of Hecate, and demanded that human sacrifices be left regularly at a certain crossroads. The peasants in the village paid in blood for almost five centuries. In return, the region remained fairly peaceful and prosperous. The village was free of outlaws, and if travelers occasionally disappeared on the road, the villagers were willing to turn a blind eye out of gratitude, and fear of the vampires and other abominations rumored to live in the castle.

In 1525, Vladimir took over management of the estate. Mihail lived to 107, and on his deathbed Hecate came to him and finally granted him immortality as a vampire in thanks for his decades of service; unfortunately, he was to spend that eternity as a very old man.

Vladimir managed the estate for nearly three centuries. Records show that between 1600 and 1800 he took at least six wives—all of whom he transformed into vampires. But after a few hundred years, he was restless and longed for travel and adventure. When war broke out through Europe in the beginning of the nineteenth century, he decided that the time had come to leave his native Romania.

In 1806, Vladimir Giurescu led Prussian troops against Napoleon, and in 1809, he led Austrian forces during the Fifth Coalition of the Napoleonic Wars. In 1811, he took part in the Battle of Redinha, and in 1812, he fought against Napoleon for control of Moscow; after the battle, Napoleon began to refer to him as "Giurescu the Devil." Though his political allegiances shifted many times during this period, Giurescu became known for his fearlessness in the field, his cruelty to captured prisoners, and the strange rituals he engaged in before and after a battle. His men respected him, and Giurescu rewarded their loyalty with wealth and women.

In 1809, Giurescu was mortally wounded during the siege of Halberstadt. Although camp doctors said that he'd be dead within the hour, his men insisted on carrying him to Castle Giurescu, where he was restored by Hecate in the light of the full moon. Two weeks later, Giurescu returned to battle. These resurrections occurred six more times in the next five years.

In 1814, Giurescu traveled to Paris to witness Napoleon's abdication. His military career over, he then traveled to the major European cities, including Zagreb, Prague, and Helsinki. Though it is known that he kept a detailed log of his travels, the log has never been recovered, and his activities from 1814 to 1880 remain shrouded in mystery.

In 1880, Giurescu arrived in England, where he apparently planned to settle in and create a new vampire family. There were rumors that he had ambitions to establish a "secret evil empire," but his plans were foiled by Sir Edward Grey, an occult detective in the service of Queen Victoria, and Giurescu barely escaped England with his life in 1882. After his narrow escape, Giurescu turned his attention back to Romania. He returned to Castle Giurescu and devoted himself to serving Hecate.

In October of 1944, Giurescu was displeased to see a delegation of Nazi agents approaching his castle on foot. He sent crows to attack them, but the birds failed to return, and he finally ventured out to investigate. Sitting beneath a tree was Ilsa Haupstein, a German agent who traveled to Romania to recruit Giurescu for the Vampir Sturm project. Above Ilsa's head perched the crows. At her feet lay the bodies of her twelve dead companions, pecked to death.

Giurescu was intrigued by Ilsa and invited her to return with him to his castle. Compared to his wives—all hundreds of years old—Ilsa seemed vitally alive, and her fearlessness impressed Giurescu. Over the following month, they fell in love, and Ilsa persuaded Giurescu to return with her to Germany, much to the displeasure of

his father—who remained in Romania—and wives—who accompanied Giurescu and Ilsa to Germany.

Nazi records show that on December 3, 1944, Giurescu met with Hitler at Wewelsburg. The next day, Giurescu and his six wives were arrested and transported to Dachau, where they were impaled, decapitated, and, allegedly, burned.

In fact, a Nazi solider had stolen Giurescu's decapitated body. The soldier sold the vampire's remains to Hans Ubler, the proprietor of a freakshow-themed nightclub popular with Himmler and his Occult Bureau. When Ubler fled Germany in 1945 to establish a wax museum in New York City, he took the body with him. In 1997, Ilsa Haupstein killed Ubler and took Giurescu's skeleton back to Castle Giurescu, where she planned to return her lover to life.

However, Ilsa Haupstein was not the only one tracking Giurescu's body. The B.P.R.D., which was investigating Ubler's murder and the theft of the skeleton, sent Hellboy to Castle Giurescu. Hellboy arrived just as Giurescu's corpse was being restored to life, and was able to stab Giurescu, but the vampire escaped into the chamber under Hecate's temple. There, Giurescu begged the goddess to restore his life one last time. She did, and Giurescu fled. Hellboy blew up the castle, destroying Hecate's body and knocking himself unconscious. The villagers near Castle Giurescu took Hellboy's body (which had been thrown from the castle in the explosion) to the crossroads and tied him to the post as an offering to Hecate. Giurescu, fully restored by the goddess's blood, attacked Hellboy, but was destroyed, releasing the piece of Hecate's spirit that had given him immortality.

The B.P.R.D. collected Giurescu's bones, but, en route to B.P.R.D. headquarters, the skeleton was stolen from an airport storage room. Some time later, the skeleton was purchased by occult-goods smuggler Igor Bromhead, who was hiding in Italy. Through necromancy, Bromhead compelled the bones to tell him what had happened to Hecate at Castle Giurescu. The knowledge provided Bromhead the means to imprison the goddess, and provided Giurescu with revenge for Ilsa's betrayal of his love, choosing loyalty to her master Rasputin instead.

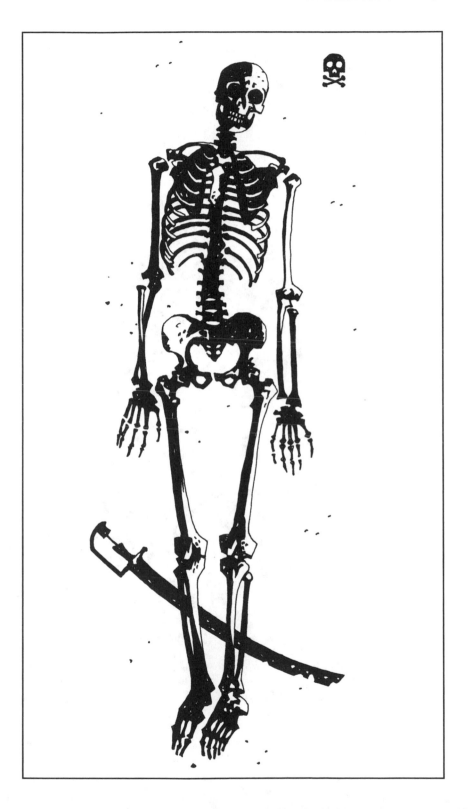

THE OFFICIAL TIMELINE

by Jason Hall

I n the beginning was the darkness, then, out of that, was born the light, and from that power all the heavenly bodies were made. And one of these was favored above all others—the earth.

And the light brought forth spirits and set them down upon the earth to watch over it, to oversee the beginning of life on that planet. But that progress proved slow, the Watchers grew impatient. They spoke thirty-two words among themselves and one raised his right hand to take fire from the air, a small piece of the power of creation. With it he formed the body of the Dragon, Ogdru Jahad, the seven who are one, and the darkness breathed into it and gave it life.

And the Ogdru Jahad delivered out of itself the three hundred and sixty-nine Ogdru Hem, the first living creatures on earth. And the Watchers were so filled with horror at the sight of the Ogdru Hem that they went to war against them—some they cast out on the wind, some they entombed in the earth, so that in the end only the Dragon remained. Then the Watcher who had dared to create it raised his right hand again, to chain it and hurl it into the abyss. Then all the other Watchers turned against that one, for fear of his power, and destroyed him and all his parts—except only for his right hand.

Then for that crime, the Watchers were taken up in a whirlwind and cast down, some upon the earth and some into the bottomless pit. Then, lesser spirits were put upon the earth and given flesh, to become the first race of men.

From *The True Secret History of the World*
by Miss Amelia Dunn (1857–1928)

THE FIRST AGE

In the sacred land of Hyperborea, covering entirely what will become the North Pole, the first prehuman race of men live in harmony with nature. Their sacred object is the hand of that destroyed watcher.

THE GOLDEN AGE

Hyperborean civilization reaches its height under Thoth, the last great king. Outposts are established in other parts of the world. Thoth has the Watcher's right hand encased in a statue that will stand in his garden for ten thousand years.

The golden age ends with the coming of Heca-Emem-Ra, later called Hecate, a woman "born out of the shadow of the moon." She seduces Thoth and profanes his temple, called Gorinium. Thoth drives her from the temple and curses her so that she is "half changed in her shape and can no more bear the light of day." Thoth dies, and one of the Ogdru Hem, called Sadu-Hem, is reborn, growing out of the blood spilled in the temple.

THE LAST AGE

Hyperborea becomes the "domain of evil men." Heca-Emem-Ra is worshipped as Neb-Ogeroth, the Black Goddess, until the statue containing the watcher's right hand comes to life to "vent its rage against the people" and it is covered in their blood. The statue then throws itself from the walls of the city and is dashed to pieces—all the pieces are lost except for its blood-red right hand. Hyperborea freezes and disappears under Polarian ice.

The survivors of Hyperborea escape to the White Island. Here they split into two tribes. The followers of the Right-Hand Path use Vril power to leave the earth and establish a new homeland in another dimension. The followers of the Left-Hand Path retreat into caverns underground. From here, they seek to control the destiny of the newly emerging human race. They also build war machines to dominate the humans when the time is right. Even-

tually, their own artificially created slave-race will rise up against them, killing them all.

After the freezing of Hyperborea, none of its outposts last long. Atlantis is the last, but without Hyperborea, it only survives a few hundred years. The few Hyperborean priests who survive remain in hiding, watching the evolution of the new race of men, and eventually teaching a chosen few to summon and control Vril power.

APPROX. 300 B.C.

Lipu Monastery, Egypt

A bronze statue of the Hindu goddess Durga instructs a monk to forge ten daggers (one for each of her arms), for the purpose of killing demons.

SOMETIME DURING THE FIRST MILLENNIUM

Menouthis, Egypt

Ini-Herit partially transcribes the great Tabula Smaragdina (the Emerald Tablet—supposedly engraved by the god Hermes on a stone that fell from the head of the first of the fallen angels when the angel was cast out of heaven), creating the text of what will be known as *Flamma Reconditus* (*The Secret Fire*), a book containing the secrets of the universe. However, shortly after Ini-Herit completes his transcription, the city is drowned—either due to earthquakes or a flood from the Nile.

554 A.D.

September

West Sussex, England (near Horsham)

A simple monk battles a dragon, driving it "back into the hollow of the earth." Lilies grow where the dragon spilled the monk's blood. The man is later dubbed St. Leonard, and the forest, St. Leonard's Wood.

964 A.D.

June

Mayfield, England

In the guise of a woman, the lesser demon Ualac attempts to seduce St. Dunstan. Dunstan uses tongs to ensnare the demon and seals him in a box, which the saint hides away.

12TH CENTURY

North America

On a small island in what will eventually be called Lake Talutah, sacrifices are made in worship to the Dragon, Ogdru Jahad, still trapped in the Abyss.

1214

June

St. August, Eastern Europe

Drawn into town by the ringing of church bells, Philip of Bayeux finds the royal Grenier family of St. August praying to an "image of the Devil Antichrist" (more likely an old fertility god). He wrecks the chapel and curses the family to become wolves every seventh year, retaining their human reason so that they will "better know the horror of [their] punishment."

1221

March

St. August, Eastern Europe

The villagers catch the Greniers in their wolf forms. The entire family is killed, except for a boy, William, who is smuggled out of the castle by a servant.

1222

Siberia

A tribe of warriors called the Chutt come down from their mountain to fight for Genghis Kahn, believing that the gods have chosen him to be the new emperor of the world.

1227

August

Siberia

After the death of Genghis Khan, the Chutt cut their hair, break their weapons, and return to their mountain, not to be heard of again for over seven hundred years.

1299

September

Piazza San Marcos, Venice, Italy

After a life of immoral indulgences (including destroying a vampire from Rome and drinking his blood), Romulus Diovanni is burned at the stake by the Knights Templar for murdering hundreds of people.

1326

St. August, Eastern Europe

To avoid the Inquisition, the town of St. August changes its name to Griart. Villagers destroy the chapel bell tower.

1332

Paris, France

A pamphlet titled *The Wolves of St. August* is published.

1491

Summer

The Duchy of Fabre, France

The castle of the Marquis Adoet de Fabre is destroyed by an angry mob and/or a sudden violent storm. The Marquis curses the town.

1492

June

Mihail Giurescu purchases the petrified body of the goddess Hecate from Greek fishermen. He restores her and builds her a new temple on the grounds of Castle Giurescu in Romania.

1495

December 12

Romania

Vladimir Giurescu is born.

1513

May

Castle Giurescu, Romania

Vladimir Giurescu, the only son of Mihail Giurescu, drowns and is restored to life by Hecate, who gives him a small part of her spirit.

1521

August 13

Tenochtitlán, South America

Cortéz conquers the Aztec city. An unnamed Spanish priest is taken into the vaults underneath the city, where over several days he is taught to read three gold tablets—a record of the "Secret History of the World."

1522

Soldiers find the unnamed Spanish priest beneath Tenochtitlán, and the gold tablets are broken and melted down (presumably taken back to Spain as gold bars), making the priest's memory the only living record of their contents. The priest is then returned to Spain and imprisoned and tortured by the Inquisition. Some months later, he is rescued by a "secret order of scholars, dedicated to the preservation of ancient wisdom," who hide him away on an island off the coast of Portugal.

1525

An island off the coast of Portugal

Soldiers of the Inquisition track down and murder the unnamed Spanish priest. However, Urgo-Hem (one of the disembodied Ogdru Hem torn from their bodies and "cast out on the wind") is reborn out of the priest's blood and traps all present for the rest of their lives. Upon his death, the priest promises to return when mankind is ready to hear about the Secret History of the World and the return of the Ogdru Hem and Ogdru Jahad.

1529

September

Wittenberg, Germany

While still a student, alchemist Edel Mischrasse secretly creates his first man-sized homunculus, using Ini-Herit's notes as a starting point. Fearing it will be discovered by the authorities, he poisons the homunculus and drops it down a well.

1533

August

Czege Castle, Romania

Mischrasse creates his second, and final, homunculus—later known as Roger.

1566

October

In Germany, Mischrasse's first homunculus wills himself back to life and searches for his creator. Finding him in France awaiting trial by the Inquisition, the homunculus murders Mischrasse and locates his notes at the Cathedral at Albi.

1574

April 30 (Walpurgis Night)

Harz Mountains, Germany

At a witches' sabbath, a sixteen-year-old English witch asks for and receives magical powers from a demon—and in that moment conceives the child who will eventually be called Hellboy.

1591

May

Ableben, France

(formerly the Duchy of Fabre)

The curse of the Marquis de Fabre is expunged by Pope Sixtus V and the people begin to rebuild the city.

Early July

The Cathedral of Sobegnon is built overnight by demons under the control of Sixtus using the power of one of King Solomon's nine rings.

1611

September

Monastery of Capatineni, Romania

Soldiers are sent to investigate rumors of monks "perpetrating the foulest abominations and filthiest excesses." They nail the doors shut and burn the monastery with the monks trapped inside.

1617

October

A church in East Bromwich, England

The English witch, having died repentant, is placed in a chained coffin by her two children, a monk and a nun. The two are incinerated while trying to save their dead mother from being claimed by the demon who had originally granted her powers in 1547. The witch is taken to hell, where she delivers the child who will eventually be called Hellboy.

1639

June 14

Saint-Sébastien, an island off the west coast of France

After years as a leper colony, the island (named after Saint Sébastien, martyred approximately 300 A.D.) is wiped out by a fire, leaving no survivors. Soon after, the French government takes over the island and builds a large church, which becomes the center of growth for the new town.

1645

April

England

Witchfinder Henry Hood's eighteen-month-long reign of terror begins, resulting in the hanging of over 260 accused witches throughout the country.

1646

October

England

Witchfinder Henry Hood's eyes are burned out with heated copper coins and he is buried alive in an unmarked grave.

1661

May

London, England

Dutch alchemist Johann Isaac Hollandus publishes *The Secret Fire*—his Latin translation of an earlier Greek translation of Ini-Herit's text.

1693

August

Shiloh, Massachusetts

Reverend Uriah Blackwood accuses Priscilla, Prudence, and Pollyanne Trask of witchcraft, testing the three sisters by binding them with chains and tossing them into a lake. They sink and drown.

1709

June 28

Poltava, Ukraine

Tsar Pyotr Alexeyevich Romanov (Peter the Great) summons a demon trinity to aid him in battle. Under their watchful eyes, Peter defeats the Swedish forces at the Battle of Poltava, solidifying the power of the Russian Empire. In payment, the first two demons take Peter's heart and the lives of his future sons. However, the third demon, who was to take Peter's soul (which was also to serve as the demon's passage home), decides to stay and walk the earth.

1729

March

Paris, France

After being introduced to the ancient mysteries by Lazrod in Egypt, Eugene Remy establishes the Heliopic Brotherhood of Ra.

1736

July

Paris, France

Members of the Heliopic Brotherhood of Ra split off and establish the Oannes Society.

1745

April

Paris, France

Eugene Remy dies and is buried in a secret tomb somewhere under the city.

1779

February 13

Suffolk, England

Elihu Cavendish is born.

1798

July 24

Charlottesville, Virginia

Langdon Everett Caul is born.

1806

Vladimir Giurescu commands Prussian troops as an officer during the Fourth Coalition of the Napoleonic Wars.

1809

Vladimir Giurescu leads Austrian forces during the Fifth Coalition of the Napoleonic Wars. Later, he is mortally wounded during the Siege of Halberstadt. His servants carry him home to Castle Giurescu in Romania, and two weeks later he rejoins his troops, back to full health. This occurs six or seven times during the war.

1810

May

Langdon Everett Caul goes to sea at the age of twelve.

1812

October

Russia

During the Sixth Coalition of the Napoleonic Wars, Vladimir Giurescu leads Cossack guerrillas against the Grande Armée retreating out of Moscow. Napoleon begins referring to him as "Giurescu the Devil."

1814

April 6

Paris, France

Vladimir Giurescu witnesses Napoleon's abdication.

1815

June 18

South of Brussels, Belgium

Vladimir Giurescu fights with Blücher and the Prussians in the Battle of Waterloo.

1817

March

Langdon Everett Caul meets Captain Elihu Cavendish and sails under him for the next sixteen years, traveling to Africa, the South China Sea, and other exotic locales.

1833

June

Caul stops sailing under Cavendish but continues to sail and begins pursuing his own "private investigations of a scientific nature."

1834

August
Paris, France
Caul is initiated into the Oannes Society.

1836

February 19
Long Island, New York
H.W. Carp is born.

1837

Elihu Cavendish makes his first attempt to reach the Arctic to search for evidence of Hyperborea. However, his ship is caught in an ice flo, and he is forced to abandon it. The subsequent struggle back to civilization costs the lives of half of Cavendish's crew.

1841

May

Upstate New York
Cavendish comes to America and builds Cavendish Hall on a small island in Lake Talutah, directly over the underground temple where the Ogdru Jahad were worshiped seven hundred years earlier. After construction is complete, he begins preparing for another expedition to the Arctic.

1847

July

Cavendish Hall, upstate New York

Cavendish dies of typhus before he can leave for another Arctic expedition. His unfulfilled quest will haunt every male of the family thereafter.

1853

April

Littleport, Rhode Island

Langdon Everett Caul dedicates himself to his private research, using family money to build a mansion on the coast. He is very specific about the construction and insists on certain odd architectural features. It takes eight years to complete.

1856

September 16

West Sussex, England

Edward Grey is born.

1857

June

London, England

The Universal Temple of the Heliopic Brotherhood of Ra is established.

1859

November 24

The Bayswater house of Lord Minnbrough, London, England

Langdon Everett Caul and his fellow members of the Oannes Society attend an unrolling of an Egyptian mummy sponsored by the Heliopic Brotherhood of Ra and performed by Lord Adam Glaren. The mummy, Panya, comes to life, and over the next few years becomes something of a celebrity under the guidance of Glaren.

1861

March

Littleport, Rhode Island

Langdon Everett Caul marries Edith Howard. He continues to pursue his private investigations, often entertaining "curious foreign gentlemen." Over the next three years, he begins to travel more, spending a great deal of time away from his wife and home.

1864

June

London, England

Lord Glaren and fellow members of the Heliopic Brotherhood of Ra confine Panya to their London manor. Although she is included in their experiments and conspiracies, she is a prisoner.

1865

February 22

Littleport, Rhode Island

Caul leaves home, never to return.

March

Atlantic Ocean

During an underwater expedition, Caul discovers an egglike artifact containing an ancient undersea entity.

Littleport, Rhode Island

Edith Caul goes mad and hurls herself into the sea. Her body is never recovered.

April 9

St. Trinian's Hospital, Washington, D.C.

In a secret basement room, Caul and four colleagues from the Oannes Society attempt

to make contact with the undersea entity in the egglike artifact. The artifact crumbles and the ghostly spirit image of an amphibious man only Caul can see appears. The spirit enters Caul and he begins to transform. In a spiritual/mystical loop, Abe Sapien's spirit has traveled back in time from his death in 2004, playing a part in his own transformation. The four men place Caul into a tank of water.

April 14
Washington, D.C.
President Abraham Lincoln is assassinated. The four men monitoring Caul's transformation at St. Trinian's Hospital mention the names Booth and Corbett—implying that they may have had something to do with Lincoln's shooting and Booth's subsequent killing at the hands of Corbett.

May 2
St. Trinian's Hospital, Washington, D.C.
The four men leave the completely transformed Caul in the tank of water and seal the basement room, planning to return "when it's safe."

1866
June
Surrey, England
Following a séance at the home of Lord Charles Burly, seven former members of the Heliopic Brotherhood of Ra form the Osiris Club.

1869
January 29
Pokrovskoe, Siberia
Grigori Yefimovich Rasputin is born.

1872
February
New York City
The Golden Lodge of the Heliopic Brotherhood of Ra is established.

1874
August
Long Island, New York
Dr. H.W. Carp, a member of the Heliopic Brotherhood, has his house built with a secret basement room.

1877

May

London, England

A group of Oxford researchers found the British Paranormal Society to investigate psychic and paranormal phenomenon using scientific methods.

1879

March

London, England

Occult investigator Edward Grey is knighted by Queen Victoria for his service as special agent to the crown.

1882

August

England

Sir Edward Grey foils a plot by visiting nobleman vampire Vladimir Giurescu to establish a secret evil empire in England.

1884

November

Sixty miles off the West Coast of France

After being sentenced to die and escaping his own hanging the year before, Dutch warlock Epke Vrooman flees England by ship. Sir Edward Grey tracks down Vrooman, unaware that one of the last surviving high priests of Atlantis also inhabits Vrooman's body. Grey stabs Vrooman with a Lipu dagger, inadvertently imprisoning the now powerless spirit of the high priest. The ship sinks with Vrooman and the dagger on board. Grey barely survives.

1886

January

New York City

Dr. H.W. Carp becomes a secret grand master in the Golden Lodge of the Heliopic Brotherhood of Ra.

1888

London, England

Sir Edward Grey is involved in the search for and capture of Jack the Ripper.

1889

Russia

Troubled by his emerging healing powers, Rasputin leaves his home in Pokrovskoe. He seeks answers at the monastery in Verkhoture, but leaves unsatisfied. During this time, he also becomes involved in the Khlysty sect of the Eastern Orthodox Church.

February

London, England

Sir Edward Grey breaks with Queen Victoria over her decision to suppress the killer's identity in the Jack the Ripper murders and establishes himself as a private occult detective.

1890

May

New York City

The Golden Lodge of the Heliopic Brotherhood of Ra closes.

August

Paris, France

The original temple of the Heliopic Brotherhood of Ra closes.

1891

April

London, England

Using newly developed powers of telepathic suggestion, Panya escapes from the Heliopic Brotherhood into the custody of Langdon Caul's former colleagues in the Oannes Society. They take her to their new secret base of operations off the coast of Balikpapan, Indonesia, where they worship her (albeit incorrectly) as the Egyptian water goddess Naunet. Although Panya is amused by their experiments and is well cared for, she is a prisoner once again.

1893

September
London, England

The Universal Temple of the Heliopic Brotherhood of Ra closes. The organization continues as a secret society.

1895

February

At age twenty-six, Rasputin begins having visions of the witch Baba Yaga, who explains that he has been chosen to be the "agent of change, father of a new millennium."

1897

May
New York City

Dr. H.W. Carp resigns his position as a Secret Grand Master of the Heliopic Brotherhood of Ra.

1900

January
Russia

The witch Baba Yaga appears in the flesh and Rasputin surrenders to her half of his soul, which she hides beneath Yggdrasil, the World Tree.

1902

March
Long Island, New York

"I GAVE HER ONE HALF OF MY SOUL, WHICH SHE HID IN THE ROOTS OF YGGDRASIL, THE WORLD TREE, SO THAT MY SPIRIT, AT LEAST, WOULD ALWAYS BE SAFE."

Dr. H.W. Carp performs a ceremony to conjure a demon. Hellboy temporarily appears, having traveled back in time from the year 1991. His blood is injected into a monkey, which transforms into a demon. All parties involved (other than Hellboy) die.

1905

April
St. Petersburg, Russia

Rasputin secures himself a position of influence in the Russian royal family through his ability to alleviate the symptoms of Tsarevich Alexei's hemophilia. Soon after their first meeting, Rasputin warns the royal family that the destinies of both Alexei and the Romanov dynasty are irrevocably linked to him.

1906

April 18
San Francisco, California
A major earthquake, possibly caused by secret experiments conducted by the Heliopic Brotherhood of Ra, strikes the city.

1908

June 30
Tunguska, Siberia
An enormous explosion, possibly caused by secret experiments conducted by the Heliopic Brotherhood of Ra, occurs in a forest.

July
London, England
Sir Edward Grey closes his practice and leaves England. His whereabouts for the next six years remain unknown.

1911

May
Long Island, New York
After living in her deceased brother's house for nine years, Dr. Carp's sister dies. The house is said to be haunted.

1913

August
Providence, Rhode Island
Medium Amelia Dunn completes her book *The True Secret History of the World*, based on information dictated to her over the course of two years of spiritual contact with a ghost who identifies himself only as William. The book is never published.

1914

April 13
New York City
Sir Edward Grey arrives in America. He establishes himself in the New York social scene and sets up practice as a private occult detective.

1915

October 11
Germany
Leopold Kurtz is born.

1916

March 3

Chicago, Illinois

During an investigation of the Knights of the Silver Star, Sir Edward Grey disappears. There is no record of his death.

December 29

St. Petersburg, Russia

Rasputin is poisoned, beaten, stabbed, and shot by Prince Felix Yusupov and thrown into the frozen Neva river. There, he hears the voice of the Ogdru Jahad calling to him. Rasputin flees Russia and spends the next twenty-one years living in isolation in a small hill town in Italy, occasionally preaching of the coming of Ragna Rok, the New Age of the Serpent—mankind's demise and rebirth.

1918

March 5

Essex, England

Trevor Bruttenholm is born.

1919

June 7

Germany

Ilsa Haupstein is born.

1928

September

Long Island, New York

Miss E.F. Riddell reports hearing Latin being spoken in the house of the late Dr. Carp. Further evidence of hauntings continues over the years.

1929

May

New York City

Theosophist Alden Albert Kern founds the New York City Explorers' Club to promote the search for evidence of Atlantis, Lemuria, Mu, and an entrance to the "Hollow Earth."

July

Kansas City, Kansas

The real Hercules performs with the Stubby Lewis Circus under the name Stromo.

1932

February
New York City
First sighting of the vigilante crime fighter The Lobster. Over the next several years, The Lobster is responsible for the deaths of more than a hundred organized crime figures, Axis spies, and saboteurs in New York City and Chicago. His trademark is a lobster claw symbol burned into the foreheads of his victims.

1935

April
The ruins of the church in East Bromwich, England
Trevor Bruttenholm begins studying the site, in an attempt to discover what took place there in the past.

July
Heinrich Himmler forms the Sonnenrad Society, also known as the Nazi Occult Bureau. Its members include Leopold Kurtz, Professor Doctor Karl Ruprect Kroenen, Professor Doctor Herman von Klempt, and Military Overseer General Klaus Werner von Krupt.

September
New York City
The Lobster battles Doctor Waxman, burning his laboratory to the ground, destroying

his life's work, and leaving him for dead. The Lobster also kills Waxman's henchmen, the Cossaro brothers.

1936

March

Himmler's Occult Bureau begins actively searching for the Secret Masters and Vril power (a powerful supernatural source of energy). Expeditions are sent to India, China, Africa, and South America. A major operation is undertaken to discover the remains of Atlantis. At least one submarine attempts to gain entrance to the "Hollow Earth" by an undersea tunnel in the Arctic.

June
Berlin, Germany
Herman von Klempt begins working on a human/machine hybrid army for Himmler. His body is destroyed in an explosion, but fellow scientists Karl Ruprect Kroenen and Leopold Kurtz are able to save von Klempt's head in a jar. After the accident, he continues research into mechanical prosthetics.

1937

March
Berlin, Germany
Ilsa Haupstein joins Heinrich Himmler's Occult Bureau at the request of Himmler himself.

June–July
Himmler learns of Rasputin's survival, seeks him out, and is impressed by his vision of a New Age of the Serpent. Himmler hires Rasputin and brings him to Germany to work for the Nazi cause. Working with the Nazi scientists he deems most rational (Ilsa Haupstein, Professor Doctor Karl Ruprect Kroenen, and Leopold Kurtz), Rasputin begins work on the Ragna Rok Project, leading to the creation of the Ragna Rok Engine.

September
Berlin, Germany
Physicist Ernst Oeming (the "Nazi Einstein") is close to developing the atomic bomb for Hitler.

October
New York City
Professor Kyriakos Gallaragas invents a device he names Anum's Fork, allowing him to harness Vril power. He incorporates the device into a prototype Vril Energy Suit (V.E.S.), which he tests with the assistance of his daughter Helena and delivery-man Jim Sacks.

November
New York City and Hoboken, New Jersey
Professor Gallaragas and his daughter Helena are kidnapped by Chutt warriors under the command of a mysterious gentleman who plans to create an army of dragons and return the Hyperborean empire from its frozen grave. At the same time, The Lobster's former nemesis Doctor Waxman, who survived their 1935 altercation, is working with the Nazis to acquire the V.E.S. and to blow up New York City. The Lobster rescues Helena, stops the Nazis, and recovers some of the

V.E.S. Professor Gallaragas and Jim Sacks are killed, though Jim is reborn as a super-powered being by way of the Vril power. The Lobster makes a dangerous enemy of the mysterious gentleman by interfering with his plans.

1938
January
New York City
The Lobster investigates a case involving the deaths of Zinco-Davis Laboratories employees.

July
London, England
Trevor Bruttenholm joins the British Paranormal Society.

1939
January
The assassination of Ernst Oeming prevents him from developing the atomic bomb. His remains are moved to Hunte Castle in Austria, where astronomers, astrologists, and mystics from all over Europe are gathering with Nazi scientists, including Professor Doctor Herman von Klempt.

Late January
Hunte Castle, Austria
The Nazi space program is underway. The Nazis plan to send Oeming's remains into space to serve as a host body for an incorporeal alien species (the disembodied Ogdru Hem).

February
Colorado
Now secretly working for the United States military, The Lobster fails to stop a Nazi saboteur from destroying a train full of American troops and scientists bound for the Manhattan Project in Los Alamos, New Mexico.

March 20 (vernal equinox)
Hunte Castle, Austria
U.S. troops and The Lobster invade the castle, discovering the Nazi space program in progress. It is believed all parties, including The Lobster, are killed in the explosion caused by the attack. Unknown to the U.S., Oeming's body is successfully sent into space, and Herman von Klempt survives the fire. However, it marks the end of the Nazi space program. The existence of The Lobster is completely denied by the U.S. government.

September
Germany
The Nazis begin recruiting physicists to replace those killed at Hunte Castle. Dr. Gunter Eiss, having just finished his Ph.D. in quantum mechanics, is assigned to Operation Himmel-Macht—the Third Reich's attempt to tap the "divine infinite" in order to win the war. As part of the project, the Robe of Christ and the Spear of Longinus are located and secured by the Fuehrer's men.

September 9
London, England
Superpowered criminal and Nazi agent the Steel Hawk (Rudolf Bergen) is captured by authorities.

1940

August

Berlin, Germany

Commander-in-Chief Hermann Göring and General Major Dr. Fritz Todt of the Luftwaffe meet with the superpowered criminal known as the Black Flame. Details of the meeting remain undisclosed, although it is suspected that the Black Flame continues to collaborate with the Nazis throughout the war.

September
New York City
Former police detective Norvell Cooper publishes the first of eight pulp-magazine stories featuring The Lobster, inventing The Lobster's fictional alter ego—wheelchair-bound millionaire Walter Johnson.

Mid-September
Kagoshima, Japan
The criminal Crimson Lotus (Yumi Daimio) gives birth to a son, Masaru. Her sister raises him while Crimson Lotus remains in the Emperor's service.

1944
March
Germany
Due to competing factions within Himmler's Occult Bureau fueled by Rasputin's competition for Hitler's favor, Project Ragna Rok is chosen over Operation Himmel-Macht and is officially launched.

September 20
Washington, D.C.
The U.S. military's experimental flight of the Flying Wing is attacked by the Black Flame.

October
Germany
Himmler proposes Project Vampir Sturm. A Nazi delegation, led by Ilsa Haupstein, is sent to Castle Giurescu in Romania to recruit Vladimir Giurescu to the war effort. A relationship develops between Haupstein and Giurescu.

December 3
Wewelsburg, Germany
Vladimir Giurescu meets with Hitler, and the next day Giurescu and his six wives are arrested.

December 16
Dachau, Germany
Giurescu and his wives are transported to a concentration camp and are executed the next day. However, one of his brides is first completely drained of blood for use in Project Vampir Sturm.

December 23
Tarmagant Island, off the coast of Scotland
To complete the Ragna Rok project, Rasputin performs a ritual intended to release the Ogdru Jahad from their prison. He is assisted by Ilsa Haupstein, Leopold Kurtz, and Professor Doctor Karl Ruprect Kroenen. The project is overseen by General Klaus Werner von Krupt, who accuses Rasputin of failure. However, Rasputin has successfully summoned to Earth the key to Ragna Rok.

The ruins of the church in East Bromwich, England
As Rasputin completes his ritual, members of the British Paranormal Society investigate the ruins of the church in East Bromwich. Trevor Bruttenholm, Professor Malcolm Frost, and Lady Cynthia Eden-Jones (England's top medium), along with U.S. soldiers under the command of Sgt. George Whitman, are present when Lady Cynthia senses the ghosts of the monk and the nun who died there in 1617. A moment later, a demon child with a stone right hand appears, and Bruttenholm names him Hellboy. One of the soldiers present is actually an alien in disguise secretly sent to kill the child, but chooses to let him live. Hellboy is taken back to America, to an air force base somewhere in New Mexico, where Bruttenholm and a group of other paranormal experts found the Bureau for Paranormal Research and Defense with funding from the United States government. Bruttenholm acts as director. The B.P.R.D. is granted custody of Hellboy.

1945

January
Ritter Institute for the Mentally Unstable, Berlin, Germany
One hundred and twenty of the strongest patients are injected with the vampire blood obtained from Giurescu's bride and frozen mid-transformation in liquid nitrogen. They are to be used as a final option if Germany falls to the Allied forces.

February
Germany
Hans Ubler, proprietor of a freakshow-themed nightclub nightclub frequented by Himmler's inner circle (including the Ragna Rok project members), flees the country, smuggling out Vladimir Giurescu's remains.

April 30
Berlin, Germany
Hitler orders General Friedrich Manstein to unfreeze the subjects of Project Vampir Sturm. Manstein, who has seen the error of the Nazis, does not carry out the order, instead sealing up the room containing the frozen vampires. He leaves a letter explaining his decision in the asylum's files.

May 7
Norway
With the surrender of the Nazi forces in Germany, Ilsa Haupstein, Leopold Kurtz, and Professor Doctor Karl Ruprect Kroenen put themselves into cryogenic stasis.

Late May
The Arctic
After the end of the war in Europe, Rasputin once again hears the voice of the Ogdru Jahad. He travels to the North Pole, and in the ruins of the Hyperborean temple Gorinium he finds Sadu-Hem—"left by the Ogdru Jahad that they might always have a foothold in the world." Rasputin places himself in a trance to commune with the Dragon and will remain here until awakened by Trevor Bruttenholm over forty-eight years later.

Summer
Hollywood, California
Actor Vic Williams portrays The Lobster in Republic Pictures' *The Phantom Jungle* and *Empire of Death*.

November

After spending most of the year traveling and doing research, Professor Malcolm Frost attempts to convince the U.S. government that Hellboy is too dangerous to live. He spends the rest of his life trying to prove his belief.

1946

January 17
Somerville, Massachusetts
Thomas Manning is born.

March
New Mexico air force base
Trevor Bruttenholm officially adopts Hellboy.

April
Colorado mountains
A secret government compound is built to house expatriate German scientists after World War II. The U.S. government's goal is to duplicate the work of Professor Gallaragas and create a new version of Anum's Fork called the Gallaragas Generator. Many relics, including the Robe of Christ and the Spear of Longinus, are transported from Germany to the facility.

May
Berlin, Germany
On the first field operation of the B.P.R.D., Trevor Bruttenholm travels to Berlin to collect data on occult operations abandoned by the Nazis after WWII. He forms a tentative alliance with the Soviet Committee for Arcane Studies and Esoteric Teachings, befriending its leader, Varvara (the current guise of the remaining demon summoned by Tsar Peter in 1709). During the mission, Bruttenholm encounters both the vampire von Konig and Nazi scientist Herman von Klempt (along with von Klempt's giant half-mechanical apes, Kriegaffes #1 and #2) for the first time. He discovers that von Klempt has taken possession of Project Vampir Sturm and resurrected the Nazi space program, with which he plans to send a rocket full of vampires to America. With the help of Varvara and American and Russian soldiers, the rocket and its cargo are destroyed midflight.

June 9
Washington, D.C.
The Steel Hawk, Crimson Lotus, and Geist (Richard Mott) are put on trial in the World Court for war crimes committed between 1942 and 1945.

Early June
Concord, California
Crimson Lotus's son Masaru Daimio emigrates to the United States with his maternal aunt.

July
The 79th United States Congress grants substantial and continuous funding to the B.P.R.D.

August 26
Oakland, California
Katherine Corrigan is born.

1947
May 12
New Mexico Air Force base
General Norton Ricker of the B.P.R.D. forces Hellboy to try pancakes for the first time.

Early June
Tanzania, Africa
Hellboy takes his first trip to Africa, accompanying Professor Trevor Bruttenholm on an investigation involving hyenas. Hellboy is separated from Bruttenholm and lost for a week on the Serengeti. Once found, he retains no memory of what transpired there.

July
Shortly after the Roswell incident, B.P.R.D. headquarters moves from the New Mexico air force base to Fairfield, Connecticut.

October
Nuremberg, Germany
General von Krupt is committed to Eisenvalt Sanitarium. He dies six months later, his body infested with beetles.

1952
May
Washington, D.C.
Dr. Gunter Eiss applies for a job with the U.S. Special Defense Department so he can be transferred to the secret government compound in the Colorado mountains in order to covertly continue his work on Operation Himmel-Macht—attempting to "open a door into the kingdom of heaven."

August 6
A special act of the United Nations grants Hellboy honorary human status. A week later, he begins working as a field agent for the B.P.R.D.

August–September
With Professor Bruttenholm, Hellboy investigates several hauntings in the United States and Canada, including a barn haunted by a giant cow.

October
Professor Malcolm Frost dies, having failed in his attempt to convince the U.S. government that Hellboy should be eliminated.

1953

February–May
British Isles
Hellboy and Professor Bruttenholm spend several months in England, Scotland, and Wales. On the Isle of Man, Hellboy and Bruttenholm investigate reports of a talking mongoose. At Calton Hill, near Edinburgh, Hellboy has his first encounter with fairies. They also visit Harry H. Middleton, an old school friend of the professor's. The three investigate the phantom hand at St. Alban and the Braunton Burrows hound.

1954

November
St. Leonard's Wood, England
The Osiris Club sends Hellboy to kill a dragon in a forest near Horsham. Lilies grow from Hellboy's spilled blood.

1955

August
Kyoto, Japan
Hellboy uses Cornelius Agrippa's Charm Against Demonic Animals on a giant vampire cat.

1956

March
Norway
Hellboy assists Professor Bruttenholm's friend and former colleague, Edmond Aickman. Aickman betrays Hellboy in an attempt to gain gold from King Vold, a giant headless ghost.

May–October
Palenque, Mexico
Hellboy's "lost weekend." He teams with three Mexican wrestler brothers to fight monsters and drink. After six months, B.P.R.D. agents are sent to bring him home.

1957

January
Near Jabalpur, India
Hellboy investigates mass killings.

1958

March
Malaysia
Hellboy investigates a penanggalan—a demon whose head separates from its body at night to kill innocent victims.

April 4
Secret government compound, Colorado mountains
Growing suspicious of Dr. Eiss (who is still secretly continuing Operation Himmel-Macht), his colleagues attempt to disarm his work, causing an explosion. Most of the German scientists involved in the Gallaragas Generator project are killed, and the lower level of the facility is sealed off.

September
B.P.R.D. Headquarters, Fairfield, Connecticut
Professor Bruttenholm resigns as bureau director but remains a field agent.

PALENQUE MEXICO - JUNE 2 1956

1959
May
Ireland
During another tour of the British Isles, Hellboy saves a stolen baby named Alice Monaghan from fairies. He also encounters Jenny Greenteeth and the changeling Gruagach. The Gruagach is eaten by Grom the War Pig, and is trapped in his body. Dagda, High King of the Tuatha Dé Danann (Irish fairies) refers to Hellboy as "Dacci Ab Jura—Heaven, Hell, and Human come together as one." A pipe-smoking goblin talks to Hellboy about the time of the fairies coming to a close.

August
Near Macapa, Brazil
Hellboy fights the head of Herman von Klempt and von Klempt's giant half-mechanical ape, Brutus (Kriegaffe #9). Brutus and von Klempt are left for dead in a fire.

November
New Guinea
Hellboy is involved in another case of mass killings.

1960
April
MacCrimmon Estate, Scotland
Hellboy faces the Nuckelavee.

1961
March
Alaska
Shortly after the burial of the real Hercules, Hellboy meets a lion girl and battles a hydra.

June
Ireland
Hellboy kills Iron Shoes, "the most bloodthirsty of the old border goblins."

November
Saybrook, Connecticut
Hellboy assists Father Edward Kelly in blessing a haunted fishing boat.

1962
April 15
Kansas City, Kansas
Elizabeth Anne Sherman is born.

May
England
Hellboy meets with medium Cynthia Eden-Jones before she dies. She pleads with him to reopen the East Bromwich investigation, but Hellboy does not.

September
Colorado mountains
The secret government compound is decommissioned.

1963

March
Norway
Hellboy investigates a series of grisly slayings being performed by trolls.

1964

March
Bereznik, Russia
Hellboy shoots out the Baba Yaga's left eye.

1965

March
Abbey of La Noe, France
Hellboy battles a strange ectoplasmic manifestation, one of the disembodied Ogdru Hem.

1967

September
Kyoto, Japan
Hellboy defeats a group of Japanese vampire heads.

1969

February
Romania
Hellboy is sent to deal with a major outbreak of vampire activity.

October
Lockmaben, Scotland
Hellboy and Professor Bruttenholm investigate witchcraft-related killings in a castle.

1973

July
Kansas City, Kansas
Liz Sherman's pyrokinetic powers go out of control, killing thirty-two people, including her parents and brother.

1974

May
B.P.R.D. Headquarters, Fairfield, Connecticut
Liz Sherman becomes a ward of the B.P.R.D.

1975

November
Budapest, Hungary
During another major outbreak of vampire activity, the vampire Countess Ilona Kakosy escapes from Hellboy.

1976

September
Baltimore, Maryland
Hellboy sees a performance by medium Mr. Tod.

1977

February
Lebanon, Tennessee
Hellboy aids Father William Schenk in the exorcism of a boy named Eric Powell, and is the only one able to understand Powell's gibberish. Father William tries to kill Hellboy because he believes Hellboy can hear the voice of evil.

1978

November
St. Trinian's Hospital, Washington, D.C.
Plumbers find the amphibious man (the transformed body of Langdon Everett Caul from 1865) in a tank of water inside a sealed basement room. Unaware of his true identity, the B.P.R.D. names him Abe Sapien.

1979

February
Portland, Oregon
Hellboy is unable to save medium Mr. Tod from an ectoplasmic manifestation (one of the disembodied Ogdru Hem).

March 2
B.P.R.D. Headquarters, Fairfield, Connecticut
B.P.R.D. scientists Dr. Cobb and Dr. Roddel prepare to dissect Abe Sapien, but he awakens with electrical stimulation. Days later, Hellboy releases Abe from the constant tests being performed, despite Professor Bruttenholm's and the scientists' objections. Shortly thereafter, Abe begins working with Hellboy on select cases as an unofficial field agent. Abe has no memory of his life as Langdon Everett Caul.

May
China
Several B.P.R.D. agents die, partly due to Hellboy's error.

June
London, England
While on an investigation involving English country goblins who are stealing arcane artifacts en route to the British Museum, Hellboy meets Dr. Anastasia Bransfield. They fall in love, and Hellboy spends nearly the next two years traveling with her on archaeological digs while taking a leave of absence from the B.P.R.D.

1980

April 6
Mount Ida, Crete, Greece
Hellboy accompanies Anastasia Bransfield to the Mediterranean. While consulting on an ongoing excavation, she is abducted by a powerful group of sorcerers called the Obsidian Danse.

April 14
Mount Ida, Crete, Greece
Hellboy rescues Anastasia before the sorcerers can sacrifice her, defeating the Obsidian Danse and taking them into custody.

May
B.P.R.D. Headquarters, Fairfield, Connecticut
Liz Sherman becomes an official B.P.R.D. field agent.

June
Corfu, Greece
The strangest night Hellboy and Anastasia ever spend together.

Winter
Chateau de Chaumont, Loir-et-Cher, France
Hellboy and Anastasia are involved in an archaeological dig that unearths the skeletal remains of three giants.

1981
February
Saint-Sébastien, an island off the west coast of France
Still an unofficial agent, Abe Sapien goes on his first mission without Hellboy, to recover the Lipu dagger left in Epke Vrooman's body by Sir Edward Grey in 1884.

Nacogdaches, Texas
Liz Sherman investigates cattle mutilations.

Early March
London, England
Hellboy decides to end his relationship with Anastasia Bransfield due to the constant disapproval of her peers. The breakup is difficult for both of them. However, Professor Bruttenholm blames Anastasia.

Mid-March
B.P.R.D. Headquarters, Fairfield, Connecticut
Abe Sapien officially becomes a B.P.R.D. field agent.

Late March
B.P.R.D. Headquarters, Fairfield, Connecticut
Hellboy returns to full-time active duty.

April
Australian outback
Hellboy and Abe Sapien investigate an outbreak of nightmares that are "driving people to madness and outright slaughter."

1982

April
B.P.R.D. Headquarters, Fairfield, Connecticut
Dr. Thomas Manning is promoted to director of field operations.

May
Near Jabalpur, India
Hellboy investigates more mass killings.

Late May
Calcutta, India
Hellboy and Abe investigate a case involving a djinn and a bull.

August 19
Prague
Hellboy battles the Vampire of Prague and causes an explosion that damages a large part of the city. During cleanup, B.P.R.D. agent Bud Waller discovers the remains of a small homunculus.

November
Yorkshire, England
Hellboy finally finds the body of the vampire Countess Ilona Kakosy and puts a stake through her heart.

1983

February
Hellboy apprehends Igor Bromhead, a black-market procurer of occult relics who came to the attention of the B.P.R.D. in the 1970s. Bromhead spends the next fifteen years in jail.

March
Hellboy investigates a case at an amusement park involving a woman with the head of a boar.

1984

June 17
Marnet, West Virginia
Humbert T. Jones is born. His ability to cure wounds with his bare hands will earn him the title "Miracle Boy."

GREECE
1983

July 4
Finland
Liz once again loses control of her powers during a mission involving Hellboy and thermite charges.

October
N.Y.U. Professor Kate Corrigan becomes a consultant to the B.P.R.D.

1986

Early May
Vermont
On a case for a Mrs. Crittendon, Hellboy battles a tentacled monster.

May
Egypt
Hellboy assists Anastasia Bransfield against the "Lost Army."

MacGoldrick Castle, Edinburgh, Scotland
Liz Sherman, Abe Sapien, and Professor Bruttenholm investigate a case involving "hungry trees."

September
Hellboy and Abe investigate a case involving the pirate Blackbeard's long-lost head.

1987

June
Rugby, North Dakota
Hellboy and Abe Sapien investigate a fanatical body collector with Nazi delusions.

1988

May
Roland Hills Cemetery, Lynchfield, Wyoming
Hellboy battles the Roland Hills Mole.

1989

May
Venice, Italy
Abe Sapien investigates a case involving vampires.

July
Long Island, New York
B.P.R.D. psychic Leslie Campbell holds a sitting at the house of the late Dr. H.W. Carp, resulting in the same findings as the previous five sittings held over the years:

"The location bears a psychic imprint due to a single act of violence or some other strong emotional trauma."

November
Scotland
Hellboy is present at the opening of the secret room at Castle Glamis.

December 24
England
Hellboy is unable to save Mrs. Hatch from her vampire daughter.

1990

February
Anonta, Ontario, Canada
Hellboy and Abe Sapien investigate a case involving a wendigo named Daryl.

April
Copenhagen Zoo, Scandinavia
Hellboy and Abe investigate a necromancer and shape-shifting water creatures.

1991

August 9
Long Island, New York
Hellboy and B.P.R.D. agent Pauline Raskin investigate the haunted house of Dr. H.W. Carp. Hellboy momentarily travels back in time to 1902, where his blood is drawn and injected into a monkey.

1992

February 29
London, England
Hellboy and Agent Pauline Raskin track down the ghoul Edward Stokes.

April
Africa
Professor Ali T. Kokman acquires a mummy from a lost city before a sandstorm seemingly wipes the city from existence. The mummy is put on display in the New York City Explorers' Club.

May
Lake Okanagan, British Columbia
While cataloging Canadian lake monsters, Hellboy and Abe Sapien fight the Ogopogo.

November
The Arctic
Professor Bruttenholm, the three Cavendish brothers (William, James, and Henry—descendants of Captain Elihu Cavendish), and explorer Sven Olafsen undertake the same arctic expedition planned by Elihu in 1841.

1993

January
The Arctic
The Cavendish Expedition disappears.

May
The Bahamas
Abe Sapien teams with B.P.R.D. psychic Garret Omatta to investigate a series of killings and is called a "fish god" by the ghost of a dead slave.

Early June
Mesquite Creek, Arizona
Hellboy fights the giant dog Anubis (once the Egyptian god of mummification) at a gas station.

Late June
Phoenix, Arizona
Hellboy assists Father Edward Kelly in performing a twelve-day exorcism that almost costs Kelly an eye.

July
The Arctic
The Cavendish Expedition is given up for lost.

August 16
New York City
Hellboy is blamed for the destruction of Professor Kokman's African mummy at the New York City Explorers' Club, resulting in his permanent expulsion.

December 23
The Arctic
Professor Bruttenholm, the Cavendish brothers, and Sven Olafsen, all still alive, discover the object of Elihu Cavendish's unfulfilled quest—the Hyperborean temple called Gorinium. There they find the long-dormant Rasputin, and the longer-dormant Sadu-Hem. Rasputin awakens and Sadu-Hem transforms Olafsen and the Cavendish brothers into

frog creatures—marking the first appearance of the new and final race of men.

1994

May 9

Brooklyn, New York

Professor Bruttenholm returns from the Arctic expedition and is killed in his home by one of the frog creatures, the transformed Cavendish brother Henry.

May 11

Cavendish Hall, upstate New York

Hellboy, Liz Sherman, and Abe Sapien investigate the circumstances surrounding Bruttenholm's death, resulting in a confrontation with Rasputin. In the underground temple below Cavendish Hall, Rasputin attempts to finally free the Ogdru Jahad from their prison by harnessing the elemental power inside Liz and channeling it through Sadu-Hem. Abe is possessed by the spirit of Elihu Cavendish and spears Rasputin through the chest with a harpoon. In outer space, a group of aliens (the same species as the one who was sent to kill Hellboy in 1944) continue to monitor the Ogdru Jahad's imprisonment. An explosion and fire destroy Cavendish Hall, seemingly destroying Sadu-Hem as well. Hellboy destroys the mortal remains of Rasputin, choosing not to hear anything about his own origins or the power Rasputin claims is inside of him.

Marnet, West Virginia

At the exact moment of Rasputin's death, ten-year-old Miracle Boy Humbert T. Jones awakens from a thirty-six-day-long trancelike coma and begins to bleed from a mysterious wound in his chest.

May 13
Essex, England

Hellboy attends Professor Bruttenholm's funeral, where he speaks to Edmond Aickman.

May 14
The ruins of the church in East Bromwich, England

For the first time, Hellboy visits the site where he originally appeared on earth. He has a dream of the incident that occurred there in 1617, and is led to believe that the English witch and the demon who were involved are his mother and father.

Mid-May
Norway

Members of the Nazi Ragna Rok project kept in frozen stasis (Haupstein, Kurtz, and Kroenen) begin to revive.

Late May

Though Hellboy shows interest in new sightings of the West Virginia Moth Man, he remains in England, roaming the countryside.

May 21
Griart, Eastern Europe
Hellboy, joined by B.P.R.D. consultant Kate Corrigan, investigates a series of mass murders (including the death of Father Kelly) related to the Grenier family of St. August. This is Kate's first field mission and the first time she sees a ghost.

May 29
Griart, Eastern Europe
The site of the mass murders is considered cleared of any spirits or ghosts by Dr. Izar Hoffman of the B.P.R.D.

June
Due to her recent ordeal with Rasputin, Liz Sherman quits the B.P.R.D. for the thirteenth time.

December
Hellboy is on the cover of *LIFE* magazine celebrating his fiftieth "birthday."

1996
Early March
The Caribbean
Roderick Zinco (head of the Zinco Corporation) meets the ghost of Rasputin, who informs Zinco about Ragna Rok and the revived members of the project in Norway.

Mid-March
Norway
Roderick Zinco presents himself to the revived members of the Ragna Rok Project and offers to bankroll a new Ragna Rok project.

April
Norway
Now funded by Zinco, Kurtz and Kroenen begin work on their Ragna Rok Army.

May
Munich
Psychic medium Johann Kraus falls in love with the spirit of a client's wife who died in

the Bosnian conflict. He manipulates the man into returning for repeat sessions in order to continue contact, but the wife's spirit realizes Johann's ploy and ends it.

1997

March

Soho, New York City

Ilsa Haupstein murders Howard Steinman (a.k.a. Hans Ubler) and retrieves the remains of Vladimir Giurescu.

Czege Castle, Romania

While searching for the remains of Vladimir Giurescu, Liz Sherman (newly returned to active duty) and a team of B.P.R.D. agents discover a man-sized homunculus (Edel Mischrasse's second). In an attempt to rid herself of her "gift," Liz transfers her elemental power to the homunculus, bringing it to life.

Castle Giurescu, Romania

Hellboy battles the revived Vladimir Giurescu and the goddess Hecate, blowing up Castle Giurescu and destroying Hecate's physical body. The ghost of Rasputin offers to make Ilsa Haupstein immortal by enclosing her in an iron maiden—a gift from the Baba Yaga. Giurescu sacrifices himself for Hecate, and the part of her spirit within him abandons his body and takes over Ilsa's iron maiden body. The new Hecate gives Hellboy a vision of the Ogdru Jahad. Hellboy learns of his destiny as the Beast of the Apocalypse, which he rejects.

A village near Castle Giurescu, Romania

Abe Sapien encounters the ghost of Rasputin, who states that Abe will be punished for his murder. The head of a Romanian priest tells Abe, "Sunken bells are tolling for thee. Out of the caverns of Num-Yabisc, dark and terrible deep, the ocean is calling her children home."

Norway

Zinco, Kurtz, and Kroenen complete their Ragna Rok Army. They are joined by the head of Herman von Klempt, and their castle/factory is destroyed in a massive explosion. All are presumed dead.

Late March
Bucharest, Romania

The skeleton of Vladimir Giurescu is stolen from an airport storage room on its way to B.P.R.D. headquarters.

April
The ruins of the Capatineni Monastery, Romania

Mischrasse's first homunculus creates a giant homunculus made of molten human flesh into which he transfers his essence, but the homunculus from Czege Castle (Mischrasse's second) destroys his elder brother with the elemental power given to

him by Liz Sherman. Without that power, Liz wastes away and dies. However, she is restored to life when the second homunculus (named Roger by Hellboy) returns the power to her, sacrificing his own life.

May
Near Macapa, Brazil
Having survived the explosion in Norway, Herman von Klempt returns to find his old colleagues dead and his secret projects in ruin.

September
Outside Ingolstadt, Germany
In his secret workshop, von Klempt builds his Kriegaffe #10 and is chosen by Rasputin to call the Nazi space capsule (launched from Hunte Castle in 1939) back to Earth, resulting in the coming of the Conqueror Worm.

November
B.P.R.D. Headquarters, Fairfield, Connecticut
Dr. Cobb and Dr. Roddel plan to dissect Roger the Homunculus, but Abe Sapien revives Roger with electricity. Subsequently, the scientists fit Roger with an eletric generator and, unknown to Hellboy and Roger, an incendiary bomb, as a failsafe device.

1998
June
B.P.R.D. Headquarters, Fairfield, Connecticut
Consultant Kate Corrigan becomes a full agent of the B.P.R.D.

July
Lizarza, Spain
Hellboy receives an ancient piece of paper with a drawing of his stone right hand from
Father Adrian Frost, son of Professor Malcolm Frost. The text is written in old Lemurian,
but translates as "Behold the Right Hand of Doom."

1999

May 17
Dugan Hill, England
Igor Bromhead steals the tongs of Saint Dunstan and a box containing the minor
demon Ualac.

May 19
Lockmaben, Scotland
Hellboy and Abe Sapien confront Igor Bromhead at the castle from the 1969 witchcraft
case. Bromhead escapes but is half turned into a lizard. While Hellboy battles Ualac, he
has a vision of King Dagda of the Fairies, the pipe-smoking goblin, and a mysterious
masked figure called Sir Edward, who have been observing Hellboy for years. Hellboy
defeats Ualac, who is turned over to Astaroth, Grand Duke of the Infernal Regions, to

be returned to hell. Astaroth tells Hellboy that there is a seat reserved for him in hell and that Hellboy's "crown of the apocalypse" will be waiting for him there.

May 20
Wiltshire, England
Hellboy and B.P.R.D. agent Kate Corrigan meet at one of the Avenbury stone circles to discuss the recent revelations about Hellboy's "purpose" on Earth.

May 21
Hurstmonceaux Castle, Sussex, England
Hellboy and Kate Corrigan observe a female ghost who rides a donkey.

June
B.P.R.D. Headquarters, Fairfield, Connecticut
Kate Corrigan is promoted to assistant director of field operations for the B.P.R.D.

Early July
Belcastel, France
Hellboy investigates Emile Bertrand, a man who pretends he's a werewolf and terrorizes little girls. Hellboy causes Bertrand to fall from a cliff to his death.

Late July
New Orleans shipping magnate Alexander Crossley asks the B.P.R.D. to intervene when several of his vessels become overrun with small blood-sucking serpents called draco volans.

August
Playtown, U.S.A. Amusement Park, Hollis, Virginia
Hellboy defeats the demon Caypór.

Sweden
Hellboy and Abe Sapien investigate what appear to be the skeletal remains of the Norse god Thor. Thor's hammer becomes fused to Hellboy's stone right hand. Hellboy enlists the aid of Bruttenholm's friend Edmond Aickman and his daughter Pernilla, but Aickman betrays Hellboy (again) and dies helping to bring about the return of the King of the Frost Giants.

2000

February
Ural Mountains, above the Arctic Circle
Having once again quit the B.P.R.D., Liz Sherman travels to a monastery in hopes of learning to control the fire within her. She becomes a student of Master Gheghen and remains at the monastery for the next two years.

November
B.P.R.D. Headquarters, Fairfield, Connecticut
Roger becomes an official B.P.R.D. field agent.

2001

February 3
NASA takes a photo of a Nazi spacecraft returning to Earth on a course for Hunte Castle.

February 5
Hunte Castle, Austria
Hellboy and Roger, guided by Laura Karnstein of the Austrian Secret Police, are sent to the ruins of the castle to intercept the returning spacecraft. Laura is revealed to be Inger von Klempt, granddaughter of Herman von Klempt. Hellboy and Roger battle von Klempt (and his Kriegaffe #10), Nazis transformed into frog creatures, and the Conqueror Worm—actually one of the disembodied Ogdru Hem. Hellboy also meets the alien who was sent to destroy him in 1944, right before the alien dies. The ghost of Rasputin tells Inger that her body (newly transformed by the "breath" of the Conqueror Worm) contains the seed of new life, a new race of men, and that Ragna Rok is not only the end of the world but a new beginning. Inger is killed by the ghost of The Lobster.

Having learned about the incendiary device inside Roger, and plagued with uncertainty about his own origins, Hellboy quits the Bureau, telling Kate Corrigan that he plans to travel to Africa.

Hecate destroys the ghost of Rasputin and reveals that after

Ragna Rok, she and Hellboy will pass into the new world together—to rule over it or to die together.

The World Tree, Yggdrasil

The Baba Yaga takes the last tiny bit of Rasputin and puts it into an acorn that she will wear around her neck, "close to my heart forever."

June 10
Bolivia

Marine Captain and Green Beret Benjamin Daimio leads a platoon on an extraction mission to rescue nuns supposedly kidnapped by the political group the True Path. Daimio and all of his men are ambushed by members of a mythical Jaguar Cult. Corporal Manuel Chaves is the sole survivor.

June 13
Virginia

Captain Daimio comes back to life in a United States military morgue, where he is told that he is the sole survivor of the Bolivia mission.

New Jersey

Eric Polanco comes back to life and is told that he is the sole survivor of the Bolivia mission.

2002

February
Chengdou, China
A thief steals an ancient occult artifact, unleashing eldritch power that consumes the souls of everyone in a hundred-mile radius and sears the souls of the dead from Bangkok to Dublin.

Heidelberg, Germany
While psychic medium Johann Kraus is out of body, communicating with the dead during a séance, the incident in Chengdou creates a backlash, killing those attending the séance and destroying Johann's body. Scientists at the B.P.R.D. design a suit to contain Johann's ectoplasmic form and he is made an official field agent.

March
B.P.R.D. Headquarters, Fairfield, Connecticut
Dr. Thomas Manning is promoted to bureau director and Kate Corrigan is promoted to director of field operations.

June
Africa
Hellboy eats a banana from a haunted banana tree and is pelted by rocks and garbage for three days by the ghost Kinyamkela.

September
Ural Mountains, above the Arctic Circle
Master Gheghen's monastery is damaged by a mysterious earthquake. All the monks are murdered and Liz Sherman's spirit is stolen from her body by survivors of an artificial Hyperborean slave race led by the King of Fear. Abe Sapien, Roger, and Johann Kraus descend into a tunnel under the monastery and rescue Liz before her elemental power can be used to revive ancient Hyperborean war machines within the hollow earth.

October
Africa
After several months of wandering aimlessly, Hellboy meets the two-hundred-year-old witch doctor Mohlomi, who leads him to the seashore. There, Hellboy is taken by three mermaid sisters to the bottom of the ocean. They deliver him to the sea-witch Bog Roosh, who plans to save the world from devastation by destroying Hellboy. Hellboy is rescued by one of the mermaid sisters, saves the souls of drowned sailors from Davy Jones's Locker, and then floats away. He will drift around underwater for over two years.

Elsewhere
King Dagda of the Fairies continues to watch over Hellboy, as Gruagach (still trapped in Grom's pig body and thirsty for revenge) argues with the mysterious Sir Edward that, with Hellboy gone, the fairies can reclaim the earth.

2003

April
Venice, Italy
Abe Sapien, Liz Sherman, Roger, and Johann Kraus investigate a problem with the city's canals. They save the Roman goddess Cloacina from the undead Romulus Diovanni, and Roger meets the demon Shax.

Early May
New York
Manuel Chaves discovers that Eric Polanco also survived the mission to Bolivia. They are both experiencing the same nightmares, and two weeks prior, Polanco had awoken in bed soaked in water and blood that was not his own.

Late May
Bolivia
Chaves and Polanco meet with a retired Army colonel who knows about their 2001 mission and tells them that locals believe they had encountered a jaguar spirit. He offers to take them to Huayna, a former priest of the Jaguar Cult. Polanco transforms into a jaguar creature, kills the colonel, and escapes. Chaves tracks down Huayna, who tells him that Polanco has become an "emissary" of the jaguar god. Huayna performs a ceremony to make Chaves invisible to the jaguar creature and gives him a special blade that can kill it. Chaves kills Polanco and later learns that there is yet another to be destroyed: Captain Daimio.

June
Shiloh, Massachusetts
Abe and Roger investigate when the bodies of the Trask sisters are discovered and Pastor Blackwell, a descendant of Reverend Uriah Blackwell (who executed the girls in 1693), is taken over by the town's "sin and denial." The three sisters get their revenge on Blackwell, trapping him at the bottom of the ocean.

July
Cottonville, Alabama
Liz and Roger investigate the ghost of the train destroyed in 1939 that was bound for the Manhattan Project and encounter the ghost of The Lobster.

August
Masonville, Pennsylvania
Abe, Liz, and Johann investigate a case involving monsters under children's beds.

September
Bolgrad, Moldavia
Abe, Johann, and B.P.R.D. Agent Rachel Turner investigate an outbreak of zombies caused by the spirit of the bloodthirsty tyrant Count Yegor Kurya.

October
Caulfield, Illinois
Abe, Liz, Johann, and Roger accidentally wake a thousand-year-old monster out for revenge against its slayer—the shaman Shonchin. In the tomb containing the monster's skeleton, Roger finds a small Hyperborean artifact, which, unbeknownst to them, was used by the ancient shaman to defeat the monster.

2004

Late May
Upstate New York
B.P.R.D. investigators discover a tiny fungus in the ruins of Cavendish Hall. They take the fungus to a laboratory in New Jersey and observe its growth.

Early July
New Jersey
A fungal manifestation of the creature Sadu-Hem escapes from the lab inside the dead body of Professor Irwin Derby.

Mid-July
Crab Point, Michigan
The Sadu-Hem/Derby fungus creature transforms the entire population of the town into frog creatures like those at Cavendish Hall and Hunte Castle. Liz, Abe, Kate,

Roger, and Johann confront Humbert Jones (the West Virginia Miracle Boy, now mysteriously aged), who was chosen to complete Rasputin's work—creating "the new and final race of men" that will replace the human race and wake the Ogdru Jahad. Johann's containment suit is shredded by frog creatures, and Abe is stabbed to death, fulfilling Rasputin's threat from seven years earlier in Romania. His spirit travels back in time to April 9, 1865, to play a part in his own "creation." Abe comes back to life with the knowledge that he was once a man named Langdon Everett Caul. While most of the Crab Point frog creatures are captured, some escape.

August–September
The frog cult quickly spreads across America.

October
Colorado mountains
Captain Benjamin Daimio (formerly special ops for the Pentagon and an informal consultant to the B.P.R.D.) joins the Bureau's Task Force as the field team's new

commander. The team is relocated to their new field office—the secret government compound closed in 1962. In a secret sub-basement, they discover Dr. Gunter Eiss, still alive after almost fifty years. Using the Robe of Christ and the Spear of Longinus, Eiss completes Operation Himmel-Macht, turning himself into a portal to allow a "seraphim" to enter this world from what he claims is the Kingdom of Heaven. Johann, assisted by the ghosts of the German scientists who died in 1958, closes the portal, and Daimio kills Eiss.

Littleport, Rhode Island

Kate Corrigan and Abe Sapien look into the history of Langdon Everett Caul, the man Abe believes he used to be. Abe visits Caul's long-abandoned house, where he meets the ghost of his former wife, Edith.

2005

March

An island off the coast of Portugal

After drifting underwater for over two years, Hellboy washes up on the shore of the island where the unnamed Spanish priest was hidden by the secret order of scholars in 1522. Hecate appears to Hellboy, telling him they are the agents of change and will be together at the ending of the world. She asks him to put the world out of its misery, but Hellboy rejects her and is then killed by Urgo-Hem (one of the disembodied Ogdru Hem). The ghost of the Spanish priest recreates himself from Hellboy's blood, and Hellboy, drawing strength from the witch doctor Mohlomi, comes back to life. The priest explains to Hellboy the creation of the Ogdru Jahad and Ogdru Hem, the fall of the Watchers, and the origin of Hellboy's stone right hand. He transforms into what Hellboy was meant to be—the Beast

of the Apocalypse. Urgo-Hem is destroyed while fighting Hellboy, and the Spanish priest is banished to hell by the ghosts of his original murderers. Hellboy sets adrift at sea in a small boat.

Africa

Mohlomi chooses to give up his life on earth and travels elsewhere with the mysterious Sir Edward.

April

Louisiana

Daimio, Roger, Liz, Johann, and a team of B.P.R.D. field troops battle a group of frog creatures. Unbeknownst to them, scientists from the Zinco Corporation acquire frog-creature tadpoles.

September
New York City
Under the orders of Landis Pope (the current C.E.O. of the Zinco Corporation), the Zinco R&D scientists acclimate their now fully grown frog creatures to him with the aid of electronic implants in the creatures' brains. The same scientists are also developing a new version of the Black Flame armor (like that of the WWII-era Nazi agent) for him to wear to control the growing army of frog creatures.

September
British Columbia
Roger leads the first of his many successful raids against the frog creatures.

December
Upstate New York
Pope assumes the mantle of the Black Flame and makes first contact with frog creatures outside of the Zinco labs.

2006

February

Handelson, Montana

Liz and Johann destroy a nest of frog creatures. Liz is given a white lotus by a mysterious old woman and immediately falls into a coma.

March

B.P.R.D. field office, Colorado mountains

Liz dreams of a mysterious gentleman who informs her that the mounting frog-creature problem is much worse than she can imagine. She then awakens from her coma and coughs up a small piece of parchment, which Research Specialist Professor O'Donnell says foretells the coming of Katha-Hem, one of the Ogdru Hem.

Outside Raith, Ontario
The Black Flame kills Roger and the B.P.R.D. soldiers under Roger's command.

Onurb Caverns, Idaho
The Black Flame assembles an enormous army of frog creatures. However he soon discovers that he is not in control of the frogs, but merely a pawn of Katha-Hem.

B.P.R.D. field office, Colorado mountains
Johann helps Liz contact the mysterious gentleman from her dream, who reveals that the key to stopping Katha-Hem lies in the small Hyperborean artifact Roger found, which once belonged to the ancient shaman Shonchin.

Lincoln, Nebraska
The B.P.R.D. battle the army of frog creatures and the giant Katha-Hem. Liz has a vision of the ancient shaman Shonchin, who shows her how to channel her power through the artifact to destroy Katha-Hem. The remaining frogs escape into a hole in the earth, taking the Black Flame with them. The B.P.R.D. begins its clean up of the disaster area shortly after.

Early April
Lincoln, Nebraska
The B.P.R.D. bomb the hole left by Katha-Hem and fill it in with the remains of the city.

April
Ableben, France
Field Director Kate Corrigan and B.P.R.D. Agent Andrew Devon meet with a book dealer, hoping to acquire a copy of *The Secret Fire*, which may hold the answer to bringing Roger back to life. Kate is kidnapped to the court of Marquis Adoet de Fabre,

and the book dealer reveals that he is Fabre himself. He offers to trade Kate's life for Roger's remains or for her "fish man," Abe Sapien. Kate cuts off Fabre's ring (once belonging to Pope Sixtus V) and frees two demons Fabre was keeping under his control. The demons exact their revenge on Fabre, a storm once again destroys the town, and Kate escapes—but without *The Secret Fire.*

B.P.R.D. field office, Colorado mountains
Johann's ectoplasmic form has a final conversation with Roger, who says goodbye. Later Roger's remains are laid to rest. A false name is engraved on his tombstone to discourage potential grave robbers.

August
Off the coast of Balikpapan, Indonesia
Abe encounters several of his former colleagues from the Oannes Society, who are planning to kill millions of people in order to save them by housing the souls in artificially created bodies under the Oannes members' control. With the help of the mummy Panya, Abe and Captain Daimio are able to foil their plan. Panya returns with them to the B.P.R.D.

B.P.R.D. field office, Colorado mountains
In place of his regular containment suit, Johann begins inhabiting one of the artificially created bodies left over from the Oannes Society's experiments in Indonesia. Panya is made an official consultant to the B.P.R.D.

Late August
B.P.R.D. Headquarters, Fairfield, Connecticut
The facility is closed down and most agents move to the Bureau's Washington, D.C., office.

September
B.P.R.D. field office, Colorado mountains
Daryl the wendigo is moved to B.P.R.D. holding facilities. Shortly thereafter, Captain Daimio transforms into a jaguar creature and kills five people, including his old comrade Manuel Chaves and Johann's new body, before freeing the wendigo. Both monsters escape into the mountains. Following the death of his body, Johann is briefly possessed by the ghost of masked hero The Lobster, who uses Johann's ectoplasm to shoot the mysterious gentleman in Liz Sherman's mind.

Johann contacts the spirits of two of Daimio's victims and learns that Daimio was possessed by the spirit of an ancient jaguar god, which Chaves had come to destroy. Chaves's spirit also tells Johann how the jaguar creature can be killed.

2007

February

Outside Castle Giurescu, Romania

A witch finds Hellboy's broken horns (left after his battle with Hecate), carving one into a crude statue of Hellboy and saving the other.

March

Lucca, Italy

Having acquired Vladimir Giurescu's skeleton, Igor Bromhead uses it to imprison Hecate and steal her power. Bromhead calls down the moon in an attempt to become king of the witches, but Hecate's powers prove too powerful for him to contain.

June
Suffolk, England
After being at sea for over two years, Hellboy's boat washes up in the seaside town of Southwold, near the house of Harry H. Middleton.

October
Countesthorpe, Leicester, England
Witches use a carving of Hellboy to summon him to their gathering, the largest ever seen,

to ask him to become their king. Hellboy declines, the witches declare war, and the Baba Yaga offers to remove Hellboy for good if the witches offer him to her. They do so, and he is transported to her world, beyond the Thrice-Nine Lands in the Thrice-Tenth Kingdom.

Beyond the Thrice-Nine Lands in the Thrice-Tenth Kingdom
The Baba Yaga sends Koshchei the Deathless after Hellboy. She promises to return Koshchei's soul and grant him death if he brings her Hellboy's eye, which she plans to use "to learn the secret workings of all things." Hellboy defeats Koshchei and returns to England. Koshchei's defeat weakens the Baba Yaga, and she learns that Hellboy is deathless and that his eye cannot be taken, but must be given.

Countesthorpe, Leicester, England
The Gruagach tells the witches that they are fading from this world, as is his kind. With their support, he and a handful of allies retrieve the imprisoned Queen of Blood, a being so powerful and dangerous that she had been dismembered and imprisoned for centuries.

December
Lucca, Italy
Having swallowed the moon, Bromhead begs Hellboy to kill him and end his suffering. Hellboy complies. With his last breath, Bromhead tells Hellboy he sees him there in Hell already, seated on a dragon at the head of an army.

England
Dagda, High King of the Tuatha Dé Danann, is killed by one of his subjects, and the Gruagach prepares to free the Queen of Blood."

THE LITERARY HERITAGE OF HELLBOY

by Stephen Weiner

THE PULPS

Hellboy is the natural convergence of many ideas, images, and stories that have been floating around Mike Mignola's head since he was a teenager haunting the dusty bookstores of the San Francisco Bay area in the 1970s. The comic-book industry had received a creative shot in the arm with the adaptation of the work of Robert E. Howard (1906–1936), and, to a lesser extent, authors Clark Ashton Smith (1893–1961) and H.P. Lovecraft (1890–1937), writers who'd attained a certain kind of fame in the 1930s, in *Weird Tales* and other pulp magazines. Marvel Comics' groundbreaking series *Conan the Barbarian*, originally written by Roy Thomas and illustrated by Barry Smith, ushered in a deluge of sword-and-sorcery comics and revived interest in the old pulps. Other adaptations included Fritz Leiber's *Fafhrd & the Gray Mouser*, a second Robert E. Howard creation, *King Kull*, and Michael Moorcock's albino warrior, *Elric*. Like many comics fans in the early 1970s, Mignola followed these retellings back to the original prose stories, many of which had recently been rereleased in paperback.

Howard's work led Mignola to Lovecraft and other pulp writers, like Clark Ashton Smith, Manly Wade Wellman, and Sax Rohmer. The pulps eventually led Mignola even further back, to the ghost-story and horror writers of the Victorian era: M.R. James, Algernon Blackwood, E.F. Benson, J. Sheridan Le Fanu, and William Hope Hodgson.

The contributions of James and his contemporaries became evident in the early part of the twentieth century, just as writers such as Robert E. Howard and Clark Ashton Smith were starting to craft their own tales. Like their predecessors, Howard and Smith drew heavily from folklore and mythology, and one particular detail those pulp writers dwelt upon was the ancient Greek notion of Hyperborea, a northern land of perfection and peace. For Howard, it became a terrible, despotic place, shunned by his noble brute Conan. Clark Ashton Smith made Hyperborea an island overseen by demonic gods, doomed to be swallowed by ice. Drawing from the pulps as well as the pseudoscientific theories of Helena Blavatsky and other occultists, Mignola developed his own Hyperborea, which has gradually come into focus in his most recent stories.

The era of the pulps also spawned the archetype of the hero epitomized by Howard's Conan. Conan's blunt, no-nonsense demeanor resonated powerfully for

Mignola. Some of that working-class style of Hellboy's character can be traced to Robert E. Howard, but Howard himself may have borrowed it from early stories of Dashiell Hammett (*The Maltese Falcon*), which appeared throughout the 1920s in the detective magazine *Black Mask*.

Howard's Conan stories also influenced the order in which the Hellboy stories unfolded. The Conan stories did not appear in chronological order, but jumped around in time—the first published Conan story features him as king of the most advanced society in the ancient world, while subsequent stories show him as a young barbarian from the wild north. The first Hellboy story was set fifty years after Hellboy's arrival on Earth, and since then, other stories have been set earlier or later, relative to Hellboy's age and level of experience. There can be no doubt of Howard's influence on Mignola—and Conan's on Hellboy: while writing a recent Conan series for Dark Horse, Mignola occasionally caught himself in the script referring to the protagonist as "Hellboy"!

Howard is far from the only pulp writer to make his mark on Mignola. Clark Ashton Smith's fantasy and horror stories dominated *Weird Tales* and other popular magazines in the 1930s. Smith's story "The Colossus of Ylourgne" appeared in the June 1934 issue of *Weird Tales*, and served as the inspiration for the Hellboy story "Almost Colossus," which turned an insignificant monster from an earlier issue into one of the most significant characters in the series.

The *Weird Tales* writer whose work left the most unmistakable mark on the Hellboy mythos is H.P. Lovecraft. Many look at Lovecraft as the successor to Edgar Allan Poe as master of the supernatural short story. Lovecraft's tales were populated by deities and monsters, distorted versions of gods from pre-Egyptian cultures, and wholly original creatures, native only to Lovecraft's imagination. He portrayed a universe full of cosmic awe and terror, in which evil forces were almost infinite.

One of Lovecraft's stories that seemed to have particularly inspired Mignola was "The Shadow Over Innsmouth," first published in 1931 and reissued as a short book in 1936. In it, the protagonist visits the fictional New England town of Innsmouth (probably based on Ipswich, Massachusetts). While there, the protagonist realizes that the people of Innsmouth have made a pact with an ancient sea god and that many people in Innsmouth are hybrids—half sea animal and half human. The townspeople chase the protagonist through the night and he escapes. Later, the hero realizes that he is in fact decended from one of the old families of Innsmouth, and is himself part sea creature. He also realizes that his destiny is to return to Innsmouth to live with the ancient sea god.

This is paralleled very clearly in *Hellboy*, as Mignola's hero acknowledges but ultimately rejects his inhuman heritage. Lovecraft's idea of watery evil is also present in Mignola's work: Hellboy's adoptive father, Professor Bruttenholm, is killed by the sons of an old sea captain, transformed into frog creaures. The alien race watching Hellboy and his human counterparts in the first Hellboy series—though barely explained, and appearing again only once, briefly, many years later—reflects the Lovecraftian motif of a vast, unknowable universe.

1970s comics adaptations would have introduced Mignola to Lester Dent, the creator of Doc Savage, the "Man of Bronze." As a character, Doc Savage had superhuman abilities similar to Superman's and the detective abilities of Sherlock Holmes. The Doc Savage stories were originally published by Street and Smith publications during the 1930s and 1940s and were being reprinted in the 1970s, as both paperbacks and comics; Mignola remains an avid collector of the novels. An Abe Sapien one-shot published in the mid-nineties bore a logo adapted from the Doc Savage logo. Hellboy himself, a nearly invulnerable version of the classic occult detective, comes across more like Doc Savage than the original, more effete occult detectives of Victorian literature.

One last character from the pulp era to influence Mignola was R.M.T. Scott and Grant Stockbridge's the Spider, whose adventures were also reprinted in paperback in the '70s. The Spider was a secret agent and one of the first true vigilantes. Although he bore some resemblance to the Shadow, the Spider was more violent, with a more exotic team of assistants. Written at first by Scott, then later by Stockbridge, the Spider appeared from 1933 to 1943 in popular publications. The influence of the Spider in Hellboy is subtly evident in Mignola's eclectic lineup of B.P.R.D. agents, and even more directly in Mignola's vintage 1930s hero The Lobster. Of all the pulp heroes mentioned in this section, the Spider was the only one who didn't make the transition to comic books in the 1970s, perhaps because the stories were too violent for the Comics Code Authority.

Acknowledging his debt to Howard, Lovecraft, Smith, and others, Mignola paid homage to the pulps that had inspired him when it was time to publish an anthology of Hellboy stories, for which he licensed the title *Weird Tales*, the pulp magazine in which so much of the earlier authors' work had originally appeared.

MYTHOLOGY, FOLKLORE, CHRISTIAN IMAGERY, AND LITERARY REFERENCES

The pulps were only one of many sources that influenced the creation of Hellboy and his world. Like his heroes Lovecraft and Howard, Mignola studied mythology, folktales, and classic literature, to which his own Catholic upbringing contributed a more personal sense of religious history. Like his discovery of Lovecraft and Howard, Mignola's introduction to mythology first came from Marvel Comics: Thor, hero of the monthly comic book *Journey into Mystery*, which began telling the Norse thunder god's stories in 1962 and was renamed *The Mighty Thor* in 1966. In issue #154 (1969), Stan Lee and Jack Kirby began a storyline about the destruction of the universe, the Norse Ragnarok, a war that would end one era and begin another. In this storyline, good and evil clashed on a cosmic scale. The Lee-Kirby *Thor* stories were only loosely based on traditional Norse mythology—they borrowed from it whenever events or characters proved useful; however, in traditional Norse mythology, Thor falls during the battle of Ragnarok while fighting the Midgard serpent, a snake encircling Earth. The Midgard serpent bears significant similarities to the Dragon, the Ogdru Jahad, and "Ragna Rok" is used in *Hellboy* to signify the battle that will bring about the destruction of the world—an event that some say will begin with Hellboy's death. Just as Thor was able to save the world in *Journey into Mystery* #157, Hellboy repeatedly wards off his own Ragna Rok. Furthermore, Thor wields his power primarily through his hammer, Mjolnir, swung by his right hand. Hellboy's right hand *is* the Right Hand of Doom, and packs a similarly destructive punch. The parallels between Thor and Hellboy have been developed further in two specific stories—first in the novel *The Bones of Giants*, in which Hellboy discovers Thor's hammer and finds it grafted to his own right hand; and again, allegorically, in the comics story *Makoma*, in which Hellboy merges with a hammer-wielding African hero and faces the great serpent at the end of time.

In addition to the similarities between Thor and Hellboy as characters, there are parallels between the ways in which their storylines evolved. In the earlier comics, Thor was very involved with people and their problems in his alter ego as the crippled doctor Don Blake. Later, he left Earth to fight evil on a grander scale, and delved more deeply into the world of fantasy and myth. This transformation took place over a period of five years, from 1962 to 1967. Hellboy followed a similar path. In 1994, Hellboy stories involved the supernatural but were firmly grounded in our world. By the end of the story *Conqueror Worm* (2001), Hellboy has left the B.P.R.D. and for the most part forsaken the world of humans, setting off on a personal quest that will immerse him in the folkloric and mythological elements of the series.

Thor is not the only figure from Norse mythology to make its way into *Hellboy*. The cosmology of *Hellboy* revolves around Yggdrasil, the World Tree in Norse mythology and a critical element in the Norse story of Ragnarok. After the final battle between good and evil, only two humans survive, protected by Yggdrasil, and are able to start a new race of humans. This is perhaps what Hecate—a Greek goddess who's become central to Mignola's stories—intends when she says she and Hellboy will be together at the end. Mignola also dips into Norse folklore to inform his brilliant short story "King Vold" (*The Right Hand of Doom*). Inspired by legends of the Flying Huntsman and the Green Giant, Mignola's story of King Vold is a powerful tale of greed and desperation. The resolution is chilling, with no hope of redemption—another Norse theme.

Pieces of other mythologies have also spilled into Hellboy's world. While coming up with the characters and mythos of *Hellboy*, Mignola borrowed many mythologies, from Greek and Russian, to South African, Egyptian, and Celtic.

Hecate has become perhaps the most significant mythological figure in *Hellboy*. Usually associated with Greek mythology, Hecate probably originated in a pre-Greek society, possibly Thracian, and was later incorporated into the Greek myths. Hecate is a complex goddess, and in the Hellboy saga, Mignola focuses on her status as Queen of the Witches. Hellboy first meets her in *Wake the Devil* as he is leaving Castle Giurescu. Mignola invokes Hecate in a traditional fashion, as the Goddess of Crossroads. But he also gives her story a new twist: Mignola's Hecate was cursed by the Hyperborean priest Thoth (whose name is borrowed from an Egyptian god), and, "half changed in her shape," is unable to withstand daylight. As Hellboy and the goddess battle, Hecate tries to convince him to give in to his destiny as the Beast of the Apocalypse. From this point on, Hecate takes on great significance in the Hellboy series. Even diminished and transformed, she constantly taunts Hellboy to join her for the end of the world, promising that their destinies are irrevocably entwined.

Another lead player in the Hellboy oeuvre is the Baba Yaga, a witch from Russian and Polish folklore. The Baba Yaga lives in a house on chicken legs, surrounded by a fence made of human bones. In the legends, she occasionally assists the pure at heart, but Mignola usually focuses on her more terrible aspect, which devours the souls of sinners and the bodies of children. (The exception to this rule is the Baba Yaga's relationship to Rasputin, in which she takes on the aspect of the wise grandmother.) Mignola's used her extensively in the Hellboy series, and depicts her in her traditional guise, as an old woman who flies around in a mortar and pestle. Her presence is often used to punctuate the climax of a story, showing that, while the battle may be won temporarily, a greater struggle lies ahead.

However, the Baba Yaga serves a different function in the recent *Darkness Calls*, summoned because the witches of the world need a leader. The series brings Hellboy to Russia, where he'll get pulled further into Russian folklore, confronting the Baba Yaga and her champion, Koshchei the Deathless.

One of the most pivotal characters in the Hellboy series hails not from folklore or mythology, but from Russian history. Grigori Rasputin (1869–1916) was a Russian mystic and a self-proclaimed healer, and an advisor to the ruling Romanov family. Controversial during his lifetime, accused of being the Antichrist, Rasputin was stabbed in 1914, but lived, further adding to his legendary status. He was finally killed in 1916 by a group of nobles bent on ending his perceived influence over Tsarina Alexandra. Mignola's Rasputin is based on the real person, but is changed to better fit the Hellboy story. Mignola expands the mythic status associated with the historical Rasputin by elevating him to an incredibly powerful force of evil. In *Hellboy*, Rasputin does not die in 1916, but hears the call of the Ogdru Jahad, and is made immortal. He manipulates the Nazis into supporting the Ragna Rok project, and brings Hellboy to Earth, intending for Hellboy to eventually serve as the agent of the Apocalypse, paving the way for the creation of a new world.

Mignola does not just pepper his tales with details borrowed from folklore—he empowers them with the ambience of mythology, as in the way he transforms Rasputin from a historical holy man, to self-proclaimed god, to tragic, inhuman husk. Mignola's stories have a folkloric quality that can make his work seem like retellings of older tales. This is deliberate: many of the *Hellboy* stories are in fact based on folktales or pieces of folklore. Mignola generally borrows from early Christian and European stories, with smatterings of Japanese, Caribbean, South American, and African lore, and his study of folklore and its themes has clearly influenced his development as a storyteller.

One important *Hellboy* story with roots in folklore is "The Corpse" (from *The Chained Coffin & Others*), based in part on the Irish tale "Teig O'Kane and the Corpse." In the legend, Teig O'Kane is a ne'er-do-well who disobeys his father. He runs into the fairy people, who tell him that he must overcome a series of obstacles to bury a corpse by sunrise. O'Kane does bury the corpse, but his experience changes him; he marries and settles down into the life his father had hoped for him. In Mignola's version, Hellboy sets out to rescue an infant stolen by the fairies, who tell him that, in exchange for the return of the child, he must bury the corpse of a Christian friend of the fairies before sunrise. Hellboy faces a series of obstacles himself, eventually succeeding in returning the child to its parents but gaining nothing for himself.

"The Nature of the Beast" (from *The Right Hand of Doom*) is a tale partly based on two slightly different legends of St. Leonard. According to one legend, Leonard was a hermit and holy man, living in the Vienne Valley in 559 A.D., who battled the Dragon of Temptation, driving it further and further into the woods until it disappeared. Other legends identify Leonard as an early saint of the Christian church, and give the dragon the name of Malitia. According to these legends the lily of the valley sprang from St. Leonard's blood when it was spilled during the battle with the dragon. Mignola draws on both tales in his own story: when asked by the Osiris Club to kill a dragon called the St. Leonard's Wyrm, Hellboy inadvertently uses a stone sword from a statue of St. Leonard to slay the dragon, and lilies grow from Hellboy's shed blood. "The Nature of the Beast" also serves as a good example of how Mignola uses Christian lore within the larger framework of his stories, drawing upon early Christian folk material in which lines between Paganism and Christianity blur.

Other stories that pull from early Christianity and saints include "The Wolves of St. August" (*The Chained Coffin & Others*) and "Box Full of Evil" (*The Right Hand of Doom*). "The Wolves of St. August" mixes pieces of legends of St. Patrick and St. Natalis, which in the *Hellboy* story are attributed to the monk Philip of Bayeux. St. Patrick is said to have turned Vereticus, a Welsh king, into a wolf, while St. Natalis cursed a prominent Irish family, turning all of its members into wolves for seven years. In Mignola's story, which takes place in the Balkans, Philip of Bayeux curses the noble family of St. August, turning them into wolves once every seven years.

"Box Full of Evil" recalls St. Dunstan, Archbishop of Winchester in 957. According to legend, a devil tempted Dunstan, who was working as a blacksmith. Dunstan seized the

devil by the nose with a pair of tongs and held it until it begged for mercy. In Mignola's version, Dunstan traps a devil in a box, which is later discovered by petty occult crook Igor Bromhead. Bromhead releases the demon, and Hellboy finds himself playing the role of St. Dunstan, trapping the devil again, this time in his stone right hand.

Christian imagery, beliefs, and symbolism saturate the Hellboy stories and are present even when they're not the focus of the individual stories. Hellboy is, after all, from hell, and stories such as "Christmas Underground" (*The Chained Coffin & Others*), which was inspired by an unidentified folktale, and "The Iron Shoes" (*The Chained Coffin & Others*) make use of the Christian church's power against supernatural threats. Throughout the Hellboy stories, old churches frequently figure prominently, and crucifixes often appear as powerful graphic images. However, by placing these stories inside centuries-old churches and recalling saints from the distant past, Mignola has found a way to use Christian beliefs and history as folklore in much the same way he uses non-Christian folklore, and to identify early Christianity as part of the ongoing struggle between order and destruction.

The Hellboy saga is also full of allusions to classic literature, such as the Shakespearean puppet play of *Hamlet*, which provides background in 'The Ghoul" (*The Dark Horse Book of the Dead*) or Ilsa's recitation of William Blake's "The Tyger" in *Wake the Devil*. In a few places, classic stories contribute directly to the plot, as in *Conqueror Worm*, which begins with a long passage from Poe's "Ligeia" and later borrows a line from Kipling's "Gunga Din"; and "The Third Wish" (*Strange Places*), which was inspired by Hans Christian Andersen's classic story "The Little Mermaid." It's interesting to note that in both *Conqueror Worm* and "The Third Wish," Mignola uses these literary works in the same way that he uses folk tales—as sources of inspiration and atmosphere rather than untouchable, canonical texts. By drawing upon literary works in this way, he gives them a new dimension, just as his stories lend half-remembered folk tales a new life.

CARTOONING, COMICS, AND FANTASY ART

Comics didn't just point Mignola toward pulp literature and ancient folklore—they also inspired him artistically. Cartoonists Jack Kirby and Bernie Wrightson, and fantasy artists Frank Frazetta and N.C. Wyeth, helped shape the unique visual techniques and storytelling that Mignola uses to bring Hellboy's world to life.

Jack Kirby, whose work on *Thor* has already been discussed in the mythology section, was the primary creative force behind many other comic-book characters that informed *Hellboy*. More than that, Kirby was a Herculean figure, injecting so many fresh ideas and so much raw, creative energy into the comics of the 1960s and 1970s

that his work alone inspired the careers of many of today's best cartoonists. Kirby was a career cartoonist, working from the late 1930s into the early 1980s. His artistic style, which focused on explosive power and motion through exaggerated fists and legs, visually defined the superheroes of the 1960s and early 1970s. In addition to *Thor*, two other Kirby superheroes have left indelible marks on Hellboy and his world: the Thing, a member of the Fantastic Four, and Captain America. *The Fantastic Four* first began in 1961, and ushered in the so-called Silver Age of superhero comics. To the Fantastic Four, superpowers were as much a curse as a blessing—now, a clichéd idea, but forty years ago, a new concept in comics. One member, Ben Grimm, the Thing, was the first tragic superhero. With his human mind trapped in a body of stone, the Thing longed to be human again. Like Hellboy, the Thing wisecracked his way through fights, looked silly in street clothes, and had a punch that could send a villain into the middle of the next issue. Captain America was a hero in World War II, fighting Nazi villains like the Red Skull. Mignola set Hellboy's origin in the 1940s to connect him to that simple notion of American good versus foreign—particularly Nazi—evil.

In many ways, Hellboy differs greatly from the Thing. Although both are nearly indestructible, the Thing lacks Hellboy's mythic origin and purpose. Although both are outcasts, Hellboy doesn't come across as tragic. Instead of struggling with his differences behind a façade of self-deprecating wisecracks, Hellboy simply ignores them.

The Fantastic Four influenced other aspects of Hellboy stories as well. *Hellboy* was originally conceived as a team book (ironically, in the *B.P.R.D.* series, Mignola finally has his team book, but without Hellboy). Like the B.P.R.D., the Fantastic Four were a team of freaks, who felt most at home with each other. And, like Hellboy and his allies, they rarely fought common criminals, such as bank robbers or petty thieves. Instead, most of the Fantastic Four's battles were waged against supervillains intent on destroying or conquering Earth.

But more important than the impact of any one Kirby story is the influence of Kirby's art. The power and raw abstraction of Kirby's work inspired Mignola to experiment to the degree that he has with the look of *Hellboy*. The widespread feet, the heavy splashes of black, the exaggerated anatomy, and the wild machinery and structures of Kirby's work have all found their way into Mignola's style and have become as much Mignola's trademarks as Kirby's. The perspective from which Kirby approached his work has also influenced Mignola. Kirby treated even the most outlandish stories and characters with gravity and respect—Mignola once commented that Kirby would attack the wildest ideas as though he were doing Shakespeare—and shows similar sincerity in his commitment to his own work.

Although Kirby's name is better known, Bernie Wrightson's art was a major influence on Mignola. As a mainstream cartoonist, Wrightson made his most important contribution in the early 1970s, when he co-created *Swamp Thing* for DC Comics with writer Len Wein. *Swamp Thing* is the story of Alec Holland, who is turned into a swamp creature as a result of an explosion that also kills Holland's wife. Swamp Thing is intelligent and sympathetic, but because of his extraordinary powers and monstrous appearance, he is blamed and hunted for the "death" of Alec Holland. Where Jack Kirby's work had stressed movement, Wrightson was a master of atmosphere. And *Swamp Thing* was not a superhero book, but a horror title with a monster as its protagonist. Because Swamp Thing had one foot in the supernatural world, witches and other supernatural beings populated his stories, and, because Swamp Thing retained Alec's humanity, he was a sympathetic character. Wrightson left *Swamp Thing* in 1974 but has continued to focus on horror, illustrating Mary Shelley's *Frankenstein* and several books by Stephen King. While parallels exist between Swamp Thing and Hellboy, they take a back seat to Wrightson's early influence on Mignola's art. Never before had a comics artist created such chilling settings, where it seemed so logical that super-natural beings would live.

Book-cover illustrators also left their mark on Mignola. One artist whose work still inspires him is N.C. Wyeth. Wyeth studied under Howard Pyle, and became one of America's best-known illustrators. He began his career at the *Saturday Evening Post*, but went on to paint covers and interior illustrations for a series of American classics such as *Treasure Island, The Yearling, The Last of the Mohicans, Robinson Crusoe, Kidnapped,* and *Robin Hood.* Wyeth's work stressed quiet passion, romanticism, and anticipation, and his sense of space informs Mignola's.

But the book-cover artist who impressed Mignola most deeply was Frank Frazetta. A child prodigy, Frazetta entered the world of comic-book illustration at the age of sixteen, and drew funny-animal stories, newspaper strips, and westerns, eventually landing at EC Comics. In 1964, he began illustrating book covers, redefining the market, changing the way people looked at paperbacks. His most significant contributions appear on the covers of a series of reprints of the same Robert E. Howard Conan stories that stirred Mignola's imagination. Frazetta's covers caused a sensation and revitalized popular interest in both fantasy art and sword-and-sorcery fiction.

Frazetta's work stresses power and unbridled sexuality. Figures explode off the page, with muscles rippling, the detail behind them swallowed by shadows and swirls of paint. Frazetta's style is so often imitated that it has become cliché, but the originals retain such freshness that even fifty years later, Frazetta gains new generations of fans.

Mignola's work is heir to the legacies of these artists and writers, as well as many others—Arthur Rackham to Vincent van Gogh, and Auguste Rodin to Lee Brown Coye—sometimes merged and modified, sometimes faithfully re-created, in such a unique and idiosyncratic way that Mignola's own work is often imitated. As with Frazetta, Howard, or Kirby, Mignola's imitators often fail to re-create the depth and the complexity that make Mignola's work so appealing in the first place. In the pages of Hellboy, Mignola has created a seamless gestalt of old pulp novels and classic comics, folklore and myth, fine art and fantasy art. His work invites a new generation of readers on a trip into the past, inspiring them to seek out the same timeless material that Mike Mignola once sought out in the dusty used bookstores around San Francisco Bay.

FURTHER READING

Readers of *Hellboy* have always responded to the way Mike's work draws on folklore, mythology, and Gothic literature. I think this is one of the most important parts of what Mike does: synthesizing these influences in a way that makes the result seem entirely his, and making the material accessible to readers who might not take the time to discover the classic material on their own. It has earned praise since the beginning of the *Hellboy* series and has led to one of the most common requests we get in the letter columns: a recommended reading list from Mike. We've addressed the request in small ways before, with informal, off-the-cuff lists as well as a seasonal ghost-story list in 1997's *Christmas Special.* Interest was further piqued when, in *The Chained Coffin* and *Right Hand of Doom* collections, Mike mentioned the authors and stories that had specifically inspired stories like "The Corpse" and "Almost Colossus." But this is the first time Mike's issued a general list of the work that's influenced him. I've always figured that the goal of the requests was either to better understand Mike's body of work, or, since so many of our readers are themselves aspiring or established storytellers, the readers' desire to give their own work a touch of what they see in Mike's. A comprehensive reading list would be impossible, because Mike's constantly expanding his library, but this list will give readers what it gave Mike: a broad starting point. Reading these books will inspire deeper research into subjects explored by Froud, Briggs, and the rest, and I encourage readers to dig further back, into the writers that inspired Hawthorne, Blackwood, and Howard. I'd also like to add that one of the best reading lists ever published was Lovecraft's essay *Supernatural Horror in Literature*, which will open up a whole world of weird fiction for *Hellboy* readers, just as it did for Mike. But here's Mike's list, in his own words . . .

—*Scott Allie*

FOLKLORE, MYTHOLOGY, AND THE OCCULT

- *The Encyclopedia of Witchcraft and Demonology*, by Rossell Hope Robbins, and *The New Larousse Encyclopedia of Mythology.* (I couldn't function without these two.)
- *The Fairy Books (Orange, Red, Green, etc.)*, edited by Andrew Lang. (The story I based "Makoma" on is in there somewhere.)
- *The Encyclopedia of Fairies and British Folktales and Legends,* by Katherine Briggs. (I use Briggs a lot, and there's a nod to her at the beginning of "The Iron Shoes.")
- *Faeries*, described and illustrated by Brian Froud and Alan Lee. (For my money, this is the most beautiful book on the subject.)

NOVELS

- *Dracula,* by Bram Stoker.
- *The Adventures of Pinocchio,* by C. Collodi.

I am mostly a short-story guy, but these two books made me into what I am today—whatever that is. *Dracula* introduced me to the world of the Gothic and supernatural, and *Pinocchio* . . . in *Pinocchio,* I discovered the insane combination of absurdist humor, horror, and tragedy that informs everything I do. I should also add to this list *The Wizard of Oz,* by L. Frank Baum (the great superhero team book) and *The Christmas Carol* (my all-time favorite ghost story).

THE PULPS

ROBERT E. HOWARD

One of the "big three" of the golden age (1920s and 30s) of *Weird Tales* magazine, and my first favorite author. He is best known as the creator of Conan, but a few of my favorite stories are:

- "Worms of the Earth" (featuring Bran Mac Morn)
- "The Valley of the Worm" (I think the best Howard stories have "worm" in the title.)
- "Hills of the Dead" and "The Footfalls Within" (Both of these feature Solomon Kane, my favorite recurring Howard character. More about him later.)

H.P. LOVECRAFT

Another of the "big three." Lovecraft's world (or mythos) of degenerate New England families, strange cults, prehuman races, demonic space gods, and (most important) a vast, unknowable universe is the most obvious literary influence on the Hellboy world. A few of his best are:

- "The Case of Charles Dexter Ward"
- "The Dunwich Horror"
- "The Shadow of Time"
- "The Dream Quest of Unknown Kadath"

This last story (actually a short novel) is one of my favorites. It doesn't really belong to his "mythos" stories but is a "dream-land" novel, one of several he wrote, inspired by the stories of Lord Dunsany—my favorite of the non-pulp early twentieth-century fantasy writers.

CLARK ASHTON SMITH

The third of the "big three." Smith is best known for his exotic fantasy stories set in Atlantis, Hyperborea, and Zothique, but probably my favorite story of his is set in medieval France—"The Colossus of Ylourgne." It's a great nuts-and-bolts giant-monster story, with one of my favorite endings of all time. It inspired my story "Almost Colossus."

SEABURY QUINN

While not considered one of the "big three," Quinn was actually the most popular author published in *Weird Tales* during its golden age. His occult detective, Jules de Grandin, appears in ninety-three stories, while almost never leaving Harrisonville, New Jersey. Many of these stories are great, some are horrible, and some are just insane, but they are all so much fun that I have to consider Grandin my favorite occult detective. In "The Malay Horror" (a particularly insane story) Grandin battles a penanggalan. "The Malay Horror" is one of only two stories I know of (not counting my own) to use that weird thing.

MANLY WADE WELLMAN

Wellman also wrote occult-detective stories for *Weird Tales*, but my favorite stories of his feature John the Balladeer (published in the *Magazine of Fantasy and Science Fiction*). They're set in the southern Appalachian mountains and draw heavily on the folklore of that region. John, like Howard's Solomon Kane, seems to wander aimlessly through the world and, more often than not, stumbles into supernatural adventures. This is certainly the formula I use in most of the short Hellboy stories, and these two characters, especially John, were probably the unconscious models for Hellboy, more than the more traditional occult detectives were.

WILLIAM HOPE HODGSON

For me, Hodgson exists as a category unto himself. While he predates the pulp guys mentioned above (he was killed in WWI), his great weird novel *The House on the Borderland* seems to belong to that school of cosmic horror Lovecraft made famous. He wrote several excellent stories featuring the occult detective Carnacki (like "The Whistling Room" and "The Hog"), but he is best known for his horror stories of the sea. His novel *The Boats of Glen Carrig*, and his Sargasso Sea stories (like "The Thing in the Weeds" and "The Voice in the Night") inspired my original (never finished) version of "The Island."

MISCELLANEOUS GHOSTS AND HORRORS

For this last bit, I will simply list some of my favorite weird and supernatural stories.

- "The Kings Betrothed" by E.T.A. Hoffmann
- "The Wondersmith" by Fitz James O'Brien
- "The Fall of the House of Usher" by Edgar Allan Poe
- "Who Knows?" by Guy de Maupassant
- "Feathertop" by Nathaniel Hawthorne
- "The Water Ghost of Harrowby Hall" by John Kendrick Bangs
- "The Listener" by Algernon Blackwood
- "Number 13" by M.R. James
- "The Room in the Tower" by E.F. Benson
- "Ghost Stories of the Tiled House" by J. Sheridan Le Fanu

While the influence of these stories on *Hellboy* may not be as obvious as that of the pulp stories listed above, trust me, it's all in there somewhere.

There you go . . .

MIKE MIGNOLA

Somewhere in Southern California

BIBLIOGRAPHY BY STORY

HELLBOY STORIES

"Mike Mignola's Hellboy." *San Diego Comic-Con Comics* #2. Dark Horse Comics: August 1993. Plot by Mike Mignola; script by John Byrne; art by Mike Mignola; lettering by uncredited; cover by Don Martin.

"Seed of Destruction." *Hellboy: Seed of Destruction* #1–4. Dark Horse Comics: March–June 1994. Plot by Mike Mignola; script by John Byrne; art by Mike Mignola; colors by Mark Chiarello; lettering by John Byrne; covers by Mike Mignola.

"Mike Mignola's Hellboy: World's Greatest Paranormal Investigator." *Mike Mignola's Hellboy: World's Greatest Paranormal Investigator* insert comic for *The Comic Buyer's Guide* #1070. Krause Publications: May 1994. Plot by Mike Mignola; script by John Byrne; art by Mike Mignola; lettering by uncredited; cover by Mike Mignola.

"The Wolves of Saint August." *Dark Horse Presents* #88–91. Dark Horse Comics: August–November 1994. Story by Mike Mignola; art by Mike Mignola; lettering by Pat Brosseau; covers by Mike Mignola; cover colors by Matthew Hollingsworth.

"Hi, My Name is Hellboy." *Celebrate Diversity* collector's edition catalog supplement. Diamond Comic Distributors: October 1994. Story by Mike Mignola; art by Mike Mignola; lettering by uncredited; cover by various.

"The Corpse, Parts 1–8 (of 12)." *Advance Comics* #75–82. Capital City Distribution: March–October 1995. Story by Mike Mignola; art by Mike Mignola; colors by Matthew Hollingsworth; lettering by Pat Brosseau; covers by various. (Note: Parts 9–12 were not published in the serial format.)

"The Chained Coffin." *Dark Horse Presents* #100–102. Dark Horse Comics: August 1995. Story by Mike Mignola; art by Mike Mignola; lettering by Pat Brosseau; cover by Bernie Wrightson; cover colors by Matthew Hollingsworth.

"The Corpse." *Hellboy: The Corpse and The Iron Shoes*. Dark Horse Comics: January 1996. Story by Mike Mignola; art by Mike Mignola; colors by Matthew Hollingsworth; lettering by Pat Brosseau; cover by Mike Mignola.

"The Iron Shoes." *Hellboy: The Corpse and The Iron Shoes*. Dark Horse Comics: January 1996. Story by Mike Mignola; art by Mike Mignola; colors by James Sinclair; lettering by Pat Brosseau; cover by Mike Mignola.

"Wake the Devil." *Hellboy: Wake the Devil* #1–5. Dark Horse Comics: June–October 1996. Story by Mike Mignola; art by Mike Mignola; colors by James Sinclair; lettering by Pat Brosseau; covers by Mike Mignola.

"Almost Colossus." *Hellboy: Almost Colossus* #1–2. Dark Horse Comics: June–July 1997. Story by Mike Mignola; art by Mike Mignola; colors by James Sinclair; lettering by Pat Brosseau; covers by Mike Mignola.

"A Christmas Underground." *Hellboy Christmas Special*. Dark Horse Comics: December 1997. Story by Mike Mignola; art by Mike Mignola; colors by James Sinclair; lettering by Pat Brosseau; cover by Gary Gianni.

"Heads." *Abe Sapien: Drums of the Dead*. Dark Horse Comics: March 1998. Story by Mike Mignola; art by Mike Mignola; colors by Dave Stewart; lettering by Pat Brosseau; cover by Mike Mignola.

"The Baba Yaga." *Hellboy: The Chained Coffin and Others* TPB. Dark Horse Books: August 1998. Story by Mike Mignola; art by Mike Mignola; colors by Dave Stewart; lettering by Pat Brosseau; cover by Mike Mignola; cover colors by Dave Stewart.

"The Right Hand of Doom." *Dark Horse Presents Annual 1998*. Dark Horse Comics: September 1998. Story by Mike Mignola; art by Mike Mignola; lettering by Pat Brosseau; cover by Mike Mignola; cover colors by Dave Stewart.

"The Vârcolac." *Dark Horse Extra* #14–19. Dark Horse Comics: August 1999–January 2000. Story by Mike Mignola; art by Mike Mignola; lettering by uncredited; covers by various.

"Goodbye, Mr. Tod." *Gary Gianni's The MonsterMen*. Dark Horse Comics: August 1999. Story by Mike Mignola; art by Mike Mignola; colors by Dave Stewart; lettering by Pat Brosseau; cover by Gary Gianni.

"Pancakes." *Dark Horse Presents Annual 1999*. Dark Horse Comics: August 1999. Story by Mike Mignola; art by Mike Mignola; lettering by Pat Brosseau; cover by various.

"Box Full of Evil." *Hellboy: Box Full of Evil* #1–2. Dark Horse Comics: August–September 1999. Story by Mike Mignola; art by Mike Mignola; colors by Dave Stewart; lettering by Pat Brosseau; covers by Mike Mignola.

"The Nature of the Beast." *Dark Horse Presents* #151. Dark Horse Comics: February 2000. Story by Mike Mignola; art by Mike Mignola; lettering by Pat Brosseau; cover by Mike Mignola; cover colors by Dave Stewart.

"King Vold." *Hellboy: The Right Hand of Doom* TPB. Dark Horse Books: April 2000. Story by Mike Mignola; art by Mike Mignola; colors by Dave Stewart; lettering by Pat Brosseau; cover by Mike Mignola.

"Conqueror Worm." *Hellboy: Conqueror Worm* #1–4. Dark Horse Comics: May–August 2001. Story by Mike Mignola; art by Mike Mignola; colors by Dave Stewart; lettering by Pat Brosseau; covers by Mike Mignola.

"The Third Wish." *Hellboy: The Third Wish* #1–2. Dark Horse Comics: July–August 2002. Story by Mike Mignola; art by Mike Mignola; colors by Dave Stewart; lettering by Clem Robins; covers by Mike Mignola.

"Dr. Carp's Experiment." *The Dark Horse Book of Hauntings* HC. Dark Horse Books: August 2003. Story by Mike Mignola; art by Mike Mignola; colors by Dave Stewart; lettering by Clem Robins; cover by Gary Gianni; cover colors by Jim Keegan.

"The Penanggalan." *Hellboy Premiere Edition*. Dark Horse Comics: March 2004. Story by Mike Mignola; art by Mike Mignola; colors by Dave Stewart; lettering by Clem Robins; cover A by Guy Davis; cover B by Mike Mignola.

"The Corpse." *Hellboy: The Corpse* special 25¢ reprint. Dark Horse Comics: March 2004. Story by Mike Mignola; art by Mike Mignola; colors by Matthew Hollingsworth; lettering by Pat Brosseau; cover by Mike Mignola; cover colors by Dave Stewart.

"The Troll Witch." *The Dark Horse Book of Witchcraft* HC. Dark Horse Books: June 2004. Story by Mike Mignola; art by Mike Mignola; colors by Dave Stewart; lettering by Clem Robins; cover by Gary Gianni; cover colors by Jim Keegan.

"The Ghoul." *The Dark Horse Book of the Dead* HC. Dark Horse Books: June 2005. Story by Mike Mignola; art by Mike Mignola; colors by Dave Stewart; lettering by Clem Robins; cover by Gary Gianni; cover colors by Jim Keegan.

"The Island." *Hellboy: The Island* #1–2, June–July 2005. Story by Mike Mignola; art by Mike Mignola; colors by Dave Stewart; lettering by Clem Robins; cover by Mike Mignola.

"Makoma, or, A Tale Told by a Mummy in the New York City Explorers' Club on August 16, 1993." *Hellboy: Makoma, or, A Tale Told by a Mummy in the New York City Explorers' Club on August 16, 1993* #1–2. Dark Horse Comics: February–March 2006. Story by Mike Mignola; art by Mike Mignola and Richard Corben; colors by Dave Stewart; lettering by Clem Robins; cover A by Mike Mignola; cover B by Richard Corben; Cover A & B colors by Dave Stewart.

"The Hydra and the Lion." *The Dark Horse Book of Monsters* HC. Dark Horse Books: November 2006. Story by Mike Mignola; art by Mike Mignola; colors by Dave Stewart; lettering by Clem Robins; cover by Gary Gianni; cover colors by Jim Keegan.

"Darkness Calls." *Hellboy: Darkness Calls* #1–6. Dark Horse Comics: April–December 2007. Story by Mike Mignola; art by Duncan Fegredo; colors by Dave Stewart; lettering by Clem Robins; covers by Mike Mignola; cover colors by Dave Stewart.

"The Vampire of Prague." *Hellboy: The Troll Witch and Others* TPB. Dark Horse Books: October 2007. Story by Mike Mignola; art by P. Craig Russell; colors by Lovern Kindzierski; lettering by Galen Showman; cover by Mike Mignola; cover colors by Dave Stewart.

"They That Go Down to the Sea in Ships." *Hellboy: They That Go Down to the Sea in Ships.* Dark Horse Comics: August 2007. Story by Mike Mignola and Joshua Dysart; art by Jason Shawn Alexander; colors by Dave Stewart; lettering by Clem Robins; cover by Mike Mignola and Dave Stewart.

"The Mole." *Hellboy: Free Comic Book Day.* Dark Horse Comics: April 2008. Story by Mike Mignola; art by Duncan Fegredo; colors by Dave Stewart; lettering by Clem Robins; cover by Mike Mignola and Dave Stewart.

"The Crooked Man." *Hellboy: The Crooked Man.* Dark Horse Comics: July–September 2008. Story by Mike Mignola; art by Richard Corben; colors by Dave Stewart; lettering by Clem Robins; covers by Richard Corben; cover colors by Dave Stewart.

B.P.R.D. STORIES

"Abe Sapien vs. Science." *Hellboy: Box Full of Evil* #2. Dark Horse Comics: September 1999. Story by Mike Mignola; pencils by Matt Smith; inks by Mike Mignola; colors by Dave Stewart; lettering by Pat Brosseau; cover by Mike Mignola.

"B.P.R.D." *Dark Horse Extra* #42–44. Dark Horse Comics: December 2001–February 2002. Story #42–43 by Christopher Golden; story #44 by Christopher Golden and Tom Sniegoski; art by Ryan Sook; colors by Dave Stewart; lettering by Dan Jackson; covers by various.

"Hollow Earth." *B.P.R.D.: Hollow Earth* #1–3. Dark Horse Comics: January–June 2002. Story by Mike Mignola, Christopher Golden, and Tom Sniegoski; art #1 by Ryan Sook; art #2 by Ryan Sook with Curtis P. Arnold; pencils #3 by Ryan Sook; inks #3 by Curtis P. Arnold; colors by Dave Stewart; lettering by Clem Robins; covers by Mike Mignola.

"The Soul of Venice." *B.P.R.D.: The Soul of Venice.* Dark Horse Comics: May 2003. Story by Miles Gunter and Michael Avon Oeming with Mike Mignola; art by Michael Avon Oeming; colors by Dave Stewart; lettering by Ken Bruzenak; cover by Michael Avon Oeming; cover colors by Matt Hollingsworth.

"Dark Waters." *B.P.R.D.: Dark Waters.* Dark Horse Comics: July 2003. Story by Brian Augustyn; art by Guy Davis; colors by Dave Stewart; lettering by Michelle Madsen; cover by Guy Davis.

"Night Train." *B.P.R.D.: Night Train.* Dark Horse Comics: September 2003. Story by Geoff Johns and Scott Kolins; art by Scott Kolins and Dave Stewart; colors by uncredited; lettering by Pat Brosseau; cover by Scott Kolins.

"There's Something under My Bed." *B.P.R.D.: There's Something under My Bed.* Dark Horse Comics: November 2003. Story by Joe Harris; pencils by Adam Pollina; inks by Guillermo Zubiaga; colors by Lee Loughridge; lettering by Pat Brosseau; cover by Adam Pollina; cover colors by Dave Stewart.

"Plague of Frogs." *B.P.R.D.: Plague of Frogs* #1–5. Dark Horse Comics: March–July 2004. Story by Mike Mignola; art by Guy Davis; colors by Dave Stewart; lettering by Clem Robins; covers by Guy Davis.

"Born Again." *Hellboy Premiere Edition.* Dark Horse Comics: March 2004. Story by John Arcudi; art by Guy Davis; colors by Dave Stewart; lettering by Clem Robins; cover A by Guy Davis; cover B by Mike Mignola; cover C (photo cover) uncredited.

"Another Day at the Office." *B.P.R.D.: The Soul of Venice & Other Stories* TPB. Dark Horse Books: August 2004. Story by Mike Mignola; art by Cameron Stewart; colors by Michelle Madsen; lettering by Michael Heisler; cover by Mike Mignola.

"The Dead." *B.P.R.D.: The Dead* #1–5. Dark Horse Comics: November 2004–March 2005. Story by Mike Mignola and John Arcudi; art by Guy Davis; colors by Dave Stewart; lettering by Clem Robins; German translations by Jon Nortz; covers by Guy Davis.

"The Black Flame." *B.P.R.D.: The Black Flame* #1–6. Dark Horse Comics: September 2005–January 2006. Story by Mike Mignola and John Arcudi; art by Guy Davis; colors by Dave Stewart; lettering by Clem Robins; covers by Mike Mignola.

"The Universal Machine." *B.P.R.D.: The Universal Machine* #1–5. Dark Horse Comics: April–August 2006. Story by Mike Mignola and John Arcudi; art by Guy Davis; colors by Dave Stewart; lettering by Clem Robins; covers by Mike Mignola.

"Garden of Souls." *B.P.R.D.: Garden of Souls* #1–5. Dark Horse Comics: March–July 2007. Story by Mike Mignola and John Arcudi; art by Guy Davis; colors by Dave Stewart; lettering by Clem Robins; covers by Mike Mignola.

"Killing Ground." *B.P.R.D.: Killing Ground* #1–5. Dark Horse Comics: August–December 2007. Story by Mike Mignola and John Arcudi; art by Guy Davis; colors by Dave Stewart; lettering by Clem Robins; covers by Mike Mignola.

"1946." *B.P.R.D.: 1946* #1–5. Dark Horse Comics: January–May 2008. Story by Mike Mignola and Josh Dysart; art by Paul Azaceta; colors by Nick Filardi; lettering by Clem Robins; cover art by Mike Mignola; cover colors by Dave Stewart.

"Revival." *MySpace Dark Horse Presents* #8–9. Dark Horse Comics: February–March 2008. Story by John Arcudi; art by Guy Davis; color by Dave Stewart; lettering by Clem Robins.

"War on Frogs." *B.P.R.D.: War on Frogs* #1. Dark Horse Comics: June 2008. Story by John Arcudi; art by Herb Trimpe; color by Dave Stewart; lettering by Clem Robins; cover art by Mike Mignola; cover colors by Dave Stewart.

"The Ectoplasmic Man." *B.P.R.D.: The Ectoplasmic Man.* Dark Horse Comics: June 2008. Story by Mike Mignola and John Arcudi; art by Ben Stenbeck; lettering by Clem Robins; cover art by Mike Mignola; cover colors by Dave Stewart.

"The Warning." B.P.R.D.: *The Warning* #1–5. Dark Horse Comics: July–November 2008. Story by Mike Mignola and John Arcudi; art by Guy Davis; colors by Dave Stewart; lettering by Clem Robins; cover pencils by Mike Mignola; cover inks by Kevin Nowlan; cover colors by Dave Stewart.

LOBSTER JOHNSON STORIES

"Killer in My Skull." *Hellboy: Box Full of Evil* #1. Dark Horse Comics: August 1999. Story by Mike Mignola; pencils by Matt Smith; inks by Ryan Sook; colors by Dave Stewart; lettering by Pat Brosseau; cover by Mike Mignola.

"The Iron Prometheus." *Lobster Johnson: The Iron Prometheus* #1–5. Dark Horse Comics: September 2007–January 2008. Story by Mike Mignola; art by Jason Armstrong; colors by Dave Stewart; lettering by Clem Robins; cover art by Mike Mignola; cover colors by Dave Stewart.

ABE SAPIEN STORIES

"Drums of the Dead." *Abe Sapien: Drums of the Dead.* Dark Horse Comics: March 1998. Story by Brian McDonald; art by Derek Thompson; colors by Jim Sinclair; lettering by Pat Brosseau; cover by Mike Mignola.

"The Drowning." *Abe Sapien: The Drowning* #1–5. Dark Horse Comics: February–June 2008. Story by Mike Mignola; art by Jason Shawn Alexander; color by Dave Stewart; lettering by Clem Robins; cover art by Mike Mignola; cover colors by Dave Stewart.

MAJOR CROSSOVER STORIES

"Faith, Part 3 (of 4)." *John Byrne's Next Men* #21. Dark Horse Comics: December 1993. Story by John Byrne; art for pgs 1–12 by John Byrne; art for pages 12–21 by Mike Mignola; colors by Matt Webb; lettering by uncredited; cover by Mike Mignola.

"Comes the Blast!" *Madman Comics* #5. Dark Horse Comics: January 1995. Story by Mike Allred; art by Mike Allred; colors by Laura Allred; lettering by Sean Konot; cover by Mike Allred.

"Freeze Play." *John Byrne's Babe 2* #2. Dark Horse Comics: April 1995. Story by John Byrne; art by John Byrne; colors by Matt Webb; lettering by uncredited; cover by Gary Cody.

"Ghost/Hellboy." *Ghost/Hellboy* #1–2. Dark Horse Comics: May–June 1996. Story by Mike Mignola; pencils by Scott Benefiel; inks by Jasen Rodriguez; colors by Pamela Rambo; lettering by Sean Konot; covers by Mike Mignola.

"Savage Dragon/Hellboy." *Savage Dragon* #34–35. Image Comics: December 1996–February 1997. Story by Erik Larsen; dialogue coaching by Mike Mignola; art by Erik Larsen; colors by Reuben Rude, Abel Mouton, Bill Zindel, Lea Rude, John Zaia, and Jose Arenas; lettering by Chris Eliopoulos; covers by Erik Larsen.

"Ancient Laughter." *Painkiller Jane/Hellboy* vol. 1, #1. Event Comics: August 1998. Story by Brian Augustyn; plot inspiration and dialogue coaching by Mike Mignola; pencils by Rick Leonardi; inks by Jimmy Palmiotti; colors by Elizabeth Lewis and Snakebite; lettering by Richard Starkings and Comicraft; cover A by Joe Quesada and Jimmy Palmiotti; cover B by Mike Mignola.

"Batman/Hellboy/Starman." *Batman/Hellboy/Starman* #1–2. DC Comics, Dark Horse Comics: January–February 1999. Story by James Robinson; art by Mike Mignola; colors by Matt Hollingsworth; lettering by Willie Schubert; cover A by Mike Mignola; cover B by Tony Harris.

"The Goon #7." *The Goon* #7. Dark Horse Comics: June 2004. Story by Eric Powell; framing sequence story by Mike Mignola; art by Eric Powell; framing sequence art by Mike Mignola; color assists by Robin Powell, Ben Cooke, and Barry Gregory; framing sequence colors by Dave Stewart; lettering by Clem Robins; cover by Mike Mignola.

WEIRD TALES STORIES

"Big-Top Hellboy." *Hellboy: Weird Tales* #1. Dark Horse Comics: February 2003. Story by John Cassaday; art by John Cassaday; colors by Dan Jackson; lettering by Dan Jackson; cover by John Cassaday; cover colors by Dan Jackson.

"Party Pooper." *Hellboy: Weird Tales* #1. Dark Horse Comics: February 2003. Story by Andi Watson; art by Andi Watson; colors by Andi Watson; lettering by Andi Watson; cover by John Cassaday; cover colors by Dan Jackson.

"Children of the Black Mound." *Hellboy: Weird Tales* #1. Dark Horse Comics: February 2003. Story by Fabian Nicieza; art by Stefano Raffaele; colors by Elena Sanjust; lettering by Michael Heisler; cover by John Cassaday; cover colors by Dan Jackson.

"Doc Hollow's Grand Vibro-Destructo Machine." *Hellboy: Weird Tales* #1–8. Dark Horse Comics: February 2003–April 2004. Story by John Cassaday; art by John Cassaday; colors #1–4 by Dan Jackson; colors #5–8 by Nick Derington; lettering #1–4 by Dan Jackson; lettering #5–8 by Jason Hvam; cover #1 by John Cassaday; cover colors #1 by Dan Jackson; cover #2 by Jason Pearson; cover colors #2 by Dave Stewart; cover #3 by Alex Maleev; cover #4 by Leinil Francis Yu; cover #5 by J.H. Williams III; cover #6 by Frank Cho; cover colors #6 by Dave Stewart; cover #7 by Phil Noto; cover #8 by Michael Wm. Kaluta.

"Flight Risk." *Hellboy: Weird Tales* #2. Dark Horse Comics: April 2003. Story by Joe Casey; art by Steve Parkhouse; colors uncredited; lettering uncredited; cover by Jason Pearson; cover colors by Dave Stewart.

"Hot." *Hellboy: Weird Tales* #2. Dark Horse Comics: April 2003. Story by Randy Stradley; art by Seung Kim; colors uncredited; lettering by Michelle Madsen; cover by Jason Pearson; cover colors by Dave Stewart.

"Curse of the Haunted Doily." *Hellboy: Weird Tales* #2, Dark Horse Comics: April 2003. Story by Mark Ricketts; art by Eric Wight; colors by Michelle Madsen; lettering by Michelle Madsen; cover by Jason Pearson; cover colors by Dave Stewart.

"Midnight Cowboy." *Hellboy: Weird Tales* #2. Dark Horse Comics: April 2003. Story by Eric Powell; art by Eric Powell; colors by Eric Powell and Robin Powell; lettering by Michelle Madsen; cover by Jason Pearson; cover colors by Dave Stewart.

"Still Born." *Hellboy: Weird Tales* #3. Dark Horse Comics: June 2003. Story by Matt Hollingsworth and Alex Maleev; art by Alex Maleev; colors by Matt Hollingsworth; lettering by Galen Showman; cover by Alex Maleev.

"Down Time." *Hellboy: Weird Tales* #3. Dark Horse Comics: June 2003. Story by Bob Fingerman; art by Bob Fingerman; colors uncredited; lettering uncredited; cover by Alex Maleev.

"Family Story." *Hellboy: Weird Tales* #3. Dark Horse Comics: June 2003. Story by Sara Ryan; art by Steve Lieber; colors by Jeff Parker; lettering by Steve Lieber; cover by Alex Maleev.

"The Dread Within." *Hellboy: Weird Tales* #4. Dark Horse Comics: August 2003. Story by Jason Pearson; art by Jason Pearson; colors by Dave Stewart; lettering by Michelle Madsen; cover by Leinil Francis Yu.

"Abe Sapien: Star of the B.P.R.D." *Hellboy: Weird Tales* #4. Dark Horse Comics: August 2003. Story by John Arcudi; art by Roger Langridge; colors uncredited; lettering uncredited; cover by Leinil Francis Yu.

"Haunted." *Hellboy: Weird Tales* #4. Dark Horse Comics: August 2003. Story by Tom Sniegoski; art by Ovi Nedelcu; colors by Ovi Nedelcu and Michelle Madsen; lettering by Michael Heisler; cover by Leinil Francis Yu.

"Love is Scarier Than Death." *Hellboy: Weird Tales* #5. Dark Horse Comics: October 2003. Story by J.H. Williams III and Haden Blackman; art by J.H. Williams III; lettering by Todd Klein; cover by J.H. Williams III.

"Cool Your Head." *Hellboy: Weird Tales* #5, Dark Horse Comics: October 2003. Story by Scott Morse; art by Scott Morse; colors uncredited; lettering uncredited; cover by J.H. Williams III.

"Shattered." *Hellboy: Weird Tales* #5. Dark Horse Comics: October 2003. Story by Ron Marz; art by Jim Starlin; colors by Dave Stewart; lettering by Michelle Madsen; cover by J.H. Williams III.

"Command Performance." *Hellboy: Weird Tales* #6. Dark Horse Comics: December 2003. Story by Will Pfeifer; art by P. Craig Russell; colors by Lovern Kindzierski; lettering by Galen Showman; cover by Frank Cho; cover colors by Dave Stewart.

"Friday." *Hellboy: Weird Tales* #6. Dark Horse Comics: December 2003. Story by Doug Petrie; art by Gene Colan; colors by Dave Stewart; lettering by Michael Heisler; cover by Frank Cho; cover colors by Dave Stewart.

"My Vacation in Hell." *Hellboy: Weird Tales* #6. Dark Horse Comics: December 2003. Story by Craig Thompson; art by Craig Thompson; colors uncredited; lettering uncredited; cover by Frank Cho; cover colors by Dave Stewart.

"A Love Story." *Hellboy: Weird Tales* #7. Dark Horse Comics: February 2004. Story by Tommy Lee Edwards; art by Tommy Lee Edwards; colors uncredited; lettering by John Workman; cover by Phil Noto.

"Theater of the Dead." *Hellboy: Weird Tales* #7. Dark Horse Comics: February 2004. Story by Jim Pascoe and Tom Fassbender; art by Simeon Wilkins; colors by David Self; lettering by Annie Parkhouse; cover by Phil Noto.

"Long Distance Caller." *Hellboy: Weird Tales* #7. Dark Horse Comics: February 2004. Story by Kev Walker; art by Kev Walker; colors uncredited; lettering by Michael Heisler; cover by Phil Noto.

"Fifteen Minutes . . ." *Hellboy: Weird Tales* #8. Dark Horse Comics: April 2004. Story by Jill Thompson; art by Jill Thompson; colors uncredited; lettering uncredited; cover by Michael Wm. Kaluta.

"Toy Soldier." *Hellboy: Weird Tales* #8. Dark Horse Comics: April 2004. Story by Akira Yoshida and Kia Asamiya; art by Kia Asamiya; colors by Dave Stewart; lettering by Clem Robins; cover by Michael Wm. Kaluta.

"Professional Help." *Hellboy: Weird Tales* #8. Dark Horse Comics: April 2004. Story by Evan Dorkin; art by Evan Dorkin; colors by Sarah Dyer; lettering by uncredited; cover by Michael Wm. Kaluta.

HELLBOY JUNIOR STORIES

"Maggots, Maggots, Everywhere." *Hellboy Junior Halloween Special.* Dark Horse Comics: October 1997. Story by Bill Wray; art by Bill Wray; colors by Bill Wray; lettering by John Costanza; cover by Bill Wray.

"The Creation of Hellboy, Jr." *Hellboy Junior Halloween Special.* Dark Horse Comics: October 1997. Story by Bill Wray and Mike Mignola; art by Mike Mignola; colors by Dave Stewart; lettering by John Costanza; cover by Bill Wray.

"The Devil Don't Smoke." *Hellboy Junior Halloween Special.* Dark Horse Comics: October 1997. Story by Mike Mignola; additional dialogue by Bill Wray; art by Mike Mignola; colors by Bill Wray; lettering by John Costanza; cover by Bill Wray.

"Hellboy Jr.'s Magical Mushroom Trip." *Hellboy Junior* #1. Dark Horse Comics: October 1999. Story by Bill Wray; art by Dave Cooper; colors uncredited; lettering uncredited; cover by Bill Wray.

"The House of Candy Pain." *Hellboy Junior* #2. Dark Horse Comics: November 1999. Story by Bill Wray; art by Hilary Barta; colors by Dave Stewart; lettering by John Costanza; cover by Hilary Barta.

"Hellboy Jr. Gets a Car." *Hellboy Junior* #2. Dark Horse Comics: November 1999. Story by Mike Mignola; art by Mike Mignola; colors by Dave Stewart; lettering by John Costanza; cover by Hilary Barta.

"Hellboy Jr. vs. Hitler." *Hellboy Junior* TPB. Dark Horse Books: January 2004. Story by Bill Wray; art by Bill Wray; colors by Dave Stewart; lettering by John Costanza; cover by Bill Wray.

BIBLIOGRAPHY BY COLLECTION

HELLBOY COLLECTIONS

VOLUME ONE—*HELLBOY: SEED OF DESTRUCTION*
Collects "Seed of Destruction," "Mike Mignola's Hellboy," and "Mike Mignola's Hellboy: World's Greatest Paranormal Investigator."

First Edition TPB: October 1994
Cover by Mike Mignola; cover colors by Matthew Hollingsworth; introduction by Robert Bloch.
ISBN 978-1-56971-038-4

First Edition Limited Edition HC with Slipcase: October 1994 imprint, March 1995 release.
Cover and slipcase art by Mike Mignola; introduction by Robert Bloch.
ISBN 978-1-56971-051-7

Second Edition TPB, Cover A: June 1997
Cover by Mike Mignola; introduction by Robert Bloch.
ISBN 978-1-56971-316-7

Second Edition TPB, Cover B: June 1997 imprint, Spring 1999 release
Cover by Mike Mignola; cover colors by Dave Stewart; introduction by Robert Bloch.
ISBN 978-1-56971-316-7

Third Edition TPB: November 2003
Cover by Mike Mignola; cover colors by Dave Stewart; introduction by Robert Bloch.
ISBN 978-1-59307-094-6

VOLUME TWO—*HELLBOY: WAKE THE DEVIL*
Collects "Wake the Devil."

First Edition TPB, Cover A: May 1997
Cover by Mike Mignola; introduction by Alan Moore.
ISBN 978-1-56971-226-9

First Edition TPB, Cover B: May 1997 imprint/Spring 1999 release
Cover by Mike Mignola; introduction by Alan Moore.
ISBN 978-1-56971-226-9

Second Edition TPB: November 2003
Cover by Mike Mignola; cover colors by Dave Stewart; introduction by Alan Moore.
ISBN 978-1-59307-095-3

VOLUME THREE—*HELLBOY: THE CHAINED COFFIN AND OTHERS*
Collects "The Corpse," "The Iron Shoes," "The Baba Yaga," "A Christmas Underground," "The Chained Coffin," "The Wolves of Saint August," and "Almost Colossus."

First Edition TPB: August 1998
Cover by Mike Mignola; cover colors by Dave Stewart; introduction by P. Craig Russell.
ISBN 978-1-56971-349-5

Second Edition TPB: November 2003
Cover by Mike Mignola; cover colors by Dave Stewart; introduction by P. Craig Russell.
ISBN 978-1-59307-091-5

VOLUME FOUR—*HELLBOY: THE RIGHT HAND OF DOOM*
Collects "Pancakes," "The Nature of the Beast," "King Vold," "Heads," "Goodbye, Mr. Tod," "The Vârcolac," "The Right Hand of Doom," and "Box Full of Evil."

First Edition TPB: April 2000
Cover by Mike Mignola
ISBN 978-1-56971-489-8

Second Edition TPB: November 2003
Cover by Mike Mignola.
ISBN 978-1-59307-093-9

VOLUME FIVE—*HELLBOY: CONQUEROR WORM*
Collects "Conqueror Worm."

First Edition TPB: February 2002
Cover by Mike Mignola, introduction by Guillermo del Toro.
ISBN 978-1-56971-699-1

Second Edition TPB: November 2003
Cover by Mike Mignola, introduction by Guillermo del Toro.
ISBN 978-1-59307-092-2

VOLUME SIX—*HELLBOY: STRANGE PLACES*
Collects "The Third Wish" and "The Island."

First Edition TPB: April 2006
Cover by Mike Mignola; introduction by Gary Gianni.
ISBN 978-1-59307-475-3

VOLUME SEVEN—*HELLBOY: THE TROLL WITCH AND OTHERS*
Collects "Dr. Carp's Experiment," "The Penanggalan," "The Troll Witch," "The Ghoul," "Makoma, or, A Tale Told by a Mummy in the New York City Explorers' Club on August 16, 1993," "The Hydra and the Lion," and "A Vampire in Prague."

First Edition TPB: October 2007
Cover by Mike Mignola; introduction by Walter Simonson.
ISBN 978-1-59307-860-7

VOLUME EIGHT—*HELLBOY: DARKNESS CALLS*
Collects "Darkness Calls."

First Edition TPB: May 2008
Cover by Mike Mignola and Duncan Fegredo; introduction by Jane Yolen.
ISBN 978-1-59307-896-6

LIBRARY EDITION VOLUME 1—*HELLBOY: SEED OF DESTRUCTION AND WAKE THE DEVIL*
Collects "Seed of Destruction," "Mike Mignola's Hellboy," "Mike Mignola's Hellboy: World's Greatest Paranormal Investigator," and "Wake the Devil."

First Edition HC: May 2008
Cover by Mike Mignola; introduction by Scott Allie.
ISBN 978-1-59307-910-9

LIBRARY EDITION VOLUME 2—*HELLBOY: THE CHAINED COFFIN, THE RIGHT HAND OF DOOM, AND OTHERS*
Collects "The Corpse," "The Iron Shoes," "The Baba Yaga," "A Christmas Underground," "The Chained Coffin," "The Wolves of Saint August," "Almost Colossus," "Pancakes," "The Nature of the Beast," "King Vold," "Heads," "Goodbye, Mr. Tod," "The Vârcolac," "The Right Hand of Doom," and "Box Full of Evil."

> First Edition HC: October 2008
> Cover by Mike Mignola.
> ISBN 978-1-59307-989-5

B.P.R.D. COLLECTIONS

VOLUME ONE—*B.P.R.D.: HOLLOW EARTH & OTHER STORIES*
Collects "Hollow Earth," "B.P.R.D.," "Killer in My Skull," "Abe Sapien vs. Science," and "Drums of the Dead."

> First Edition TPB: January 2003
> Cover by Mike Mignola.
> ISBN 978-1-56971-862-9

> Second Edition TPB: July 2004
> Cover by Mike Mignola.
> ISBN 978-1-56971-862-9

VOLUME TWO—*B.P.R.D.: THE SOUL OF VENICE & OTHER STORIES*
Collects "The Soul of Venice," "Dark Waters," "Night Train," "There's Something under My Bed," and "Another Day at the Office."

> First Edition TPB: August 2004
> Cover by Mike Mignola.
> ISBN 978-1-59307-132-5

VOLUME THREE—*B.P.R.D.: PLAGUE OF FROGS*
Collects "Plague of Frogs."

> First Edition TPB: January 2005
> Cover by Mike Mignola.
> ISBN 978-1-59307-288-9

VOLUME FOUR—*B.P.R.D.: THE DEAD*
Collects "Born Again" and "The Dead."

> First Edition TPB: September 2005
> Cover by Mike Mignola.
> ISBN 978-1-59307-380-0

VOLUME FIVE—*B.P.R.D.: THE BLACK FLAME*
Collects "The Black Flame."

> First Edition TPB: July 2006
> Cover by Mike Mignola.
> ISBN 978-1-59307-550-7

VOLUME SIX—*B.P.R.D.: THE UNIVERSAL MACHINE*
Collects "The Universal Machine."

First Edition TPB: January 2007
Cover by Mike Mignola; epilogue by Mike Mignola (uncredited).
ISBN 978-1-59307-710-5

VOLUME SEVEN—*B.P.R.D.: THE GARDEN OF SOULS*
Collects "Garden of Souls."

First Edition TPB: January 2008
Cover by Mike Mignola.
ISBN 978-1-59307-882-9

VOLUME EIGHT: *B.P.R.D.: KILLING GROUND*
Collects "Killing Ground."

First Edition TPB: May 2008
Cover by Mike Mignola.
ISBN 978-1-59307-956-7

VOLUME NINE: *B.P.R.D.: 1946*
Collects "1946."

First Edition TPB: November 2008
Cover by Mike Mignola.
ISBN 978-1-59582-191-1

LOBSTER JOHNSON COLLECTIONS

LOBSTER JOHNSON: THE IRON PROMETHEUS
Collects "The Iron Prometheus."

First Edition TPB: June 2008
Cover by Mike Mignola.
ISBN 978-1-59307-975-8

ABE SAPIEN COLLECTIONS

ABE SAPIEN: THE DROWNING
Collects "The Drowning."

First Edition TPB: October 2008
Cover by Mike Mignola.
ISBN 978-1-59582-185-0

WEIRD TALES COLLECTIONS

HELLBOY: WEIRD TALES, VOLUME ONE
Collects "Midnight Cowboy," "Haunted," "Family Story," "Hot," "Children of the Black Mound," "Big-Top Hellboy," "Flight Risk," "Downtime," "Abe Sapien: Star of the B.P.R.D.," "Curse of the Haunted Doily," "The Dread Within," "Still Born," and "Party Pooper."

First Edition TPB: November 2003
Cover by Mike Mignola; cover colors by Dave Stewart; introduction by Scott Allie.
ISBN 978-1-56971-622-9

HELLBOY: WEIRD TALES, VOLUME TWO

Collects "My Vacation in Hell," "A Love Story," "Shattered," "Friday," "Command Performance," "Love is Scarier Than Death," "Theater of the Dead," "Toy Soldier," "Professional Help," "Fifteen Minutes . . . ," "Long Distance Caller," "Cool Your Head," and "Doc Hollow's Grand Vibro-Destructo Machine."

First Edition TPB: October 2004
Cover by Mike Mignola; cover colors by Dave Stewart; introduction by Scott Allie.
ISBN 978-1-56971-953-4

HELLBOY JUNIOR COLLECTIONS

HELLBOY JUNIOR

Collects "The Creation of Hellboy, Jr.," "Maggots, Maggots, Everywhere," "The Devil Don't Smoke," "Hellboy Jr.'s Magical Mushroom Trip," "The House of Candy Pain," "Hellboy Jr. vs Hitler," and "Hellboy Jr. Gets a Car." (Note: this volume also contains the following non-Hellboy-related stories: "Wheezy the Sick Little Witch," "The Ginger Beef Boy," "Somnambo the Sleeping Giant," "The Wolvertons," "Squid of Man," "Sparky Bear," and "Huge Retarded Duck.")

First Edition TPB: January 2004
Cover by Bill Wray, introduction by Steve Niles.
ISBN 978-1-56971-988-6

HELLBOY™

by MIKE MIGNOLA

SEED OF DESTRUCTION
with John Byrne
ISBN: 978-1-59307-094-6 | $17.95

WAKE THE DEVIL
ISBN: 978-1-59307-095-3 | $17.95

THE CHAINED COFFIN AND OTHERS
ISBN: 978-1-59307-091-5 | $17.95

THE RIGHT HAND OF DOOM
ISBN: 978-1-59307-093-9 | $17.95

CONQUEROR WORM
ISBN: 978-1-59307-092-2 | $17.95

STRANGE PLACES
ISBN: 978-1-59307-475-3 | $17.95

THE TROLL WITCH AND OTHERS
with Richard Corben and P. Craig Russell
ISBN: 978-1-59307-860-7 | $17.95

DARKNESS CALLS
with Duncan Fegredo
ISBN: 978-1-59307-896-6 | $19.95

B.P.R.D.: HOLLOW EARTH & OTHER STORIES
by Mignola, Chris Golden, Ryan Sook, and others
ISBN: 978-1-56971-862-9 | $17.95

B.P.R.D.: THE SOUL OF VENICE & OTHER STORIES
by Mignola, Mike Oeming, Guy Davis, Scott Kolins, Geoff Johns, and others
ISBN: 978-1-59307-132-5 | $17.95

B.P.R.D.: PLAGUE OF FROGS
by Mignola and Guy Davis
ISBN: 978-1-59307-288-9 | $17.95

B.P.R.D.: THE DEAD
by Mignola, John Arcudi, and Guy Davis
ISBN: 978-1-59307-380-0 | $17.95

B.P.R.D.: THE BLACK FLAME
by Mignola, Arcudi, and Davis
ISBN: 978-1-59307-550-7 | $17.95

B.P.R.D.: THE UNIVERSAL MACHINE
by Mignola, Arcudi, and Davis
ISBN: 978-1-59307-710-5 | $17.95

B.P.R.D.: GARDEN OF SOULS
by Mignola, Arcudi, and Davis
ISBN: 978-1-59307-882-9 | $17.95

B.P.R.D.: KILLING GROUND
by Mignola, Arcudi, and Davis
ISBN: 978-1-59307-956-7 | $17.95

To find a comics shop in your area, call 1-888-266-4226. For more information or to order direct: •On the web: darkhorse.com •Email: mailorder@darkhorse.com •Phone: 1-800-862-0052 Mon.–Fri. 9 AM to 5 PM Pacific Time.